New Quilts from an Old Favorite

Orange Peel

edited by
Linda Baxter Lasco

AQS Publishing

Thank You Sponsors

Clover

JANOME

moda

Located in Paducah, Kentucky, the American Quilter's Society (AQS) is dedicated to promoting the accomplishments of today's quilters. Through its publications and events, AQS strives to honor today's quiltmakers and their work and to inspire future creativity and innovation in quiltmaking.

Executive Book Editor: Andi Milam Reynolds

Editor: Linda Baxter Lasco

Copy Editor: Chrystal Abhalter

Graphic Design: Lynda Smith

Cover Design: Michael Buckingham

Photography: Charles R. Lynch

Attention Photocopying Service: Please note the following—Publisher and authors give permission to print pages 15, 32, 40–41, 74–75, 79, 86, and 88–92 for personal use only.

Additional copies of this book may be ordered from the American Quilter's Society, PO Box 3290, Paducah, KY 42002-3290, or online at www.American-Quilter.com.

Text © 2011, American Quilter's Society

Artwork © 2011, American Quilter's Society

Library of Congress Cataloging-in-Publication Data

Lasco, Linda Baxter.
  Orange peel : new quilts from an old favorite / by Linda Baxter Lasco.
    p. cm.
  ISBN 978-1-57432-682-6
  1. Patchwork--Patterns. 2. Quilting--Patterns. 3. Quilting--Competitions--United States. I. Title.
  TT835.L363 2011
  746.46--dc22
                        2011007873

Cover: ORANGE BLOSSOM SPECIAL, detail. Full quilt page 11.

Title Page: JUICY FRUIT, details. Full quilt page 71.

Above: OH, THE WEB WE WEAVE, detail. Full quilt page 51.

Dedication

This book is dedicated to all those who see a traditional quilt block and can visualize both its link to the past and its bridge to the future.

"Honoring Today's Quilter"

THE NATIONAL QUILT MUSEUM

The National Quilt Museum (NQM) is an exciting place where the public can learn more about quilts, quiltmaking, and quiltmakers, and experience quilts that inspire and delight.

The museum celebrates today's quilts and quiltmakers through exhibits of quilts from the museum's collection and selected temporary exhibits. By providing a variety of workshops and other programs, The National Quilt Museum helps to encourage, inspire, and enhance the development of today's quilter.

Whether presenting new or antique quilts, the museum promotes understanding of and respect for all quilts—contemporary and antique, classical and innovative, machine made and handmade, utility and art.

Contents

Preface

Although preservation of the past is one of a museum's primary functions, its greatest service is performed as it links the past to the present and to the future. With that goal in mind, The National Quilt Museum sponsors an annual contest and exhibit–*New Quilts from an Old Favorite* (NQOF).

Created both to acknowledge our quiltmaking heritage and to recognize innovation, creativity, and excellence, the contest challenges today's quiltmakers to interpret a single traditional quilt block in a new and exciting work of their own design. Each year contestants respond with a myriad of stunning interpretations.

Orange Peel: New Quilts from an Old Favorite is a collection of these interpretations. You'll find a brief description of the 2012 contest, followed by the five award winners and thirteen additional finalists and their quilts.

Full-color photographs of the quilts accompany each quiltmaker's comments—comments that provide insight into their widely diverse creative processes. Patterns for the traditional Orange Peel block are included to give you a starting point for your own rendition. The winners' and finalists' tips, techniques, and patterns offer an artistic framework for your own work. A list of resources and information about The National Quilt Museum are included.

Our wish is that *Orange Peel: New Quilts from an Old Favorite* will further our quiltmaking heritage as new quilts based on the Orange Peel block are inspired by the outstanding quilts in this book.

Left: STAINED GLASS APPEAL, detail. Full quilt page 35.

The Contest

Quilts entered in the New Quilts from an Old Favorite contest must be recognizable in some way as a variation of the selected traditional block. The quilts must be no larger than 80" and no smaller than 50" on a side. Each quilt must be quilted. Quilts may only be entered by the maker(s) and must have been completed after December 31 two years prior to the entry date.

Quiltmakers are asked to send in two images—one of the full quilt and one detail shot—for jurying. Three jurors view these images and consider technique, artistry, and interpretation of the theme block to select 18 finalists from among all the entries. These finalist quilts are then sent to the museum where a panel of three judges carefully evaluates them. The evaluation of the actual quilts focuses on design, innovation, theme, and workmanship. The first- through fifth-place winners are selected and notified.

An exhibit of all the winning and finalist quilts opens at The National Quilt Museum in Paducah each spring, then travels to venues around the country for two years. Thousands of quilt enthusiasts have enjoyed these exhibits nationwide.

A book is produced by the American Quilter's Society featuring full-color photos of all the quilts, biographical information about each quilter, and tips, techniques, and patterns used in making the quilts. The book provides an inside look at how quilts are created and a glimpse into the artistic mindset of today's quiltmakers.

Previous theme blocks have been Double Wedding Ring, Log Cabin, Ohio Star, Mariner's Compass, Pineapple, Kaleidoscope, Storm at Sea, Bear's Paw, Tumbling Blocks, Feathered Star, Monkey Wrench, Seven Sisters, Dresden Plate, Rose of Sharon, Sawtooth, Burgoyne Surrounded, and Sunflower. The Baskets block has been selected for the 2012 contest. Jacobs's Ladder and Carolina Lily will be the featured blocks for the 2013 and 2014 contests.

NQM would like to thank this year's sponsors: Janome America, Inc.; Clover Needlecraft, Inc.; and Moda Fabrics.

Left: HOLA MOLA, detail. Full quilt page 43.

The Orange Peel Block

What quilt block pattern comes to mind when you hear the name Orange Peel? In *The Encyclopedia of Pieced Quilt Patterns*[1], there are six patterns named Orange Peel[2]. Of these six, four share that configuration with up to nine other block names such as Orange Slices, the Reel, and Rob Peter and Pay Paul. In order to tease out some meaning of the history of the block, 56 quilts from the Quilt Index[3] and three from the International Quilt Study Center[4] were analyzed. The majority were made in the date ranges of 1850–1875 and 1930–1949. Ladies Art Company of St. Louis[5], credited with being the first mail-order quilt pattern company, included an Orange Peel pattern in their first catalog published in 1895 or possibly as early as 1889[6]. It would seem that quilters used the Orange Peel pattern long before the pattern companies published it under that name.

With the sample Orange Peel quilts being concentrated in the 1850–1875 and 1930–1949 ranges, a few theories come to mind as to the pattern's popularity. Was this, then, a pattern that simply went in and out of fashion? Mountain Mist, which has published quilt patterns since the 1920s, did not issue an Orange Peel pattern. They did issue a pattern for Robbing Peter to Pay Paul: #103[7]. Was it possible that this other name for the same pattern was more popular? A search of the Quilt Index and the IQSC online collections uncovered 34 quilts with patterns the same as Orange Peel but called Robbing Peter to Pay Paul, about half of the number as under the name Orange Peel. This might reflect the preferences of the examiners who collected the data for these collections and not reflect the pattern name the quilt was known by at the time of its creation.

As is typical for antique quilts, the names we know them by today may not be what they were called by their makers. The colonial revival began with the Philadelphia Centennial Exposition of 1876, and publishers found a market for colonial quilt patterns that would allow the maker to keep up with style. In reality, the quilt patterns touted as "colonial" rarely were: the predominant quilt styles during the colonial period were wholecloth and medallion, and the patterns marketed as "colonial" were block-style. Marketing, however, is not a science based on reality but an art based on perception. Thus, the quilt names and patterns published from 1876 to the 1930s were intended to appeal to an awakening sense of the United States as a country, and not a history lesson.

Oranges were a rare treat in the nineteenth century. Only the wealthy would have had access to oranges on any kind of regular basis. The name "Orange Peel" does not seem exotic to us in this age of refrigeration but to the quiltmaker of 1895 it certainly was. The lack of oranges in everyday life is an indication either that the name was unknown to quiltmakers before publishers dreamed it up, or that it was so exotic that it *was* used as a name, bringing a touch of the tropics into a quiltmaker's day-to-day existence. Robbing Peter to Pay Paul would have been a concept already known, and using the pattern called by that name was considered to be instructive.

Of the 59 quilts studied, 43 were referred to as "two-color," with the pattern rendered as a positive-negative with two fabrics, not necessarily two solids, and often with one of the fabrics being printed. Ten of the 59 quilts in the sample were scrap-style, ranging from 1850 to 1953. In *Clues in the Calico: A Guide to Identifying and Dating Antique Quilts*[8], Brackman provides date ranges of 1840–1925 for Turkey red and white quilts[9] and 1830–1930 for blue and white quilts[10]. Of the red and white two-color Orange Peel quilts there were four, ranging from 1880 to 1920. There were seven blue and white Orange Peel quilts in the sample, ranging from 1850 to 1935. These date ranges are consistent with Brackman's date ranges. Yet it is puzzling that a pattern so obviously suited to being pieced in blue or red plus white is not found more frequently in those combinations.

Exotically named, yet simple in construction, the Orange Peel block has provided nearly two centuries of quiltmakers with inspiration for stitching.

Judy Schwender
Curator of Collections/Registrar
The National Quilt Museum

1. Barbara Brackman, *Encyclopedia of Pieced Quilt Patterns*. (Paducah, Kentucky: American Quilter's Society, 1993).
2. Ibid., #207, #1519, #1527, #2683, #3110, #3539.
3. The Quilt Index, accessed December 17 and December 20, 2010, http://www.quiltindex.org.
4. International Quilt Study Center & Museum: Collections, accessed December 17 and December 20, 2010, http://www.quiltstudy.org/collections/search.html.
5. *Encyclopedia of Pieced Quilt Patterns*, 524.
6. Ibid., 198.
7. Xenia Cord, e-mail message to author, December 17, 2010.
8. Barbara Brackman, *Clues in the Calico: A Guide to Identifying and Dating Antique Quilts*.(McLean, Virginia: EPM Publications, 1989).
9. Brackman, Clues, 157.
10. Ibid., 158.

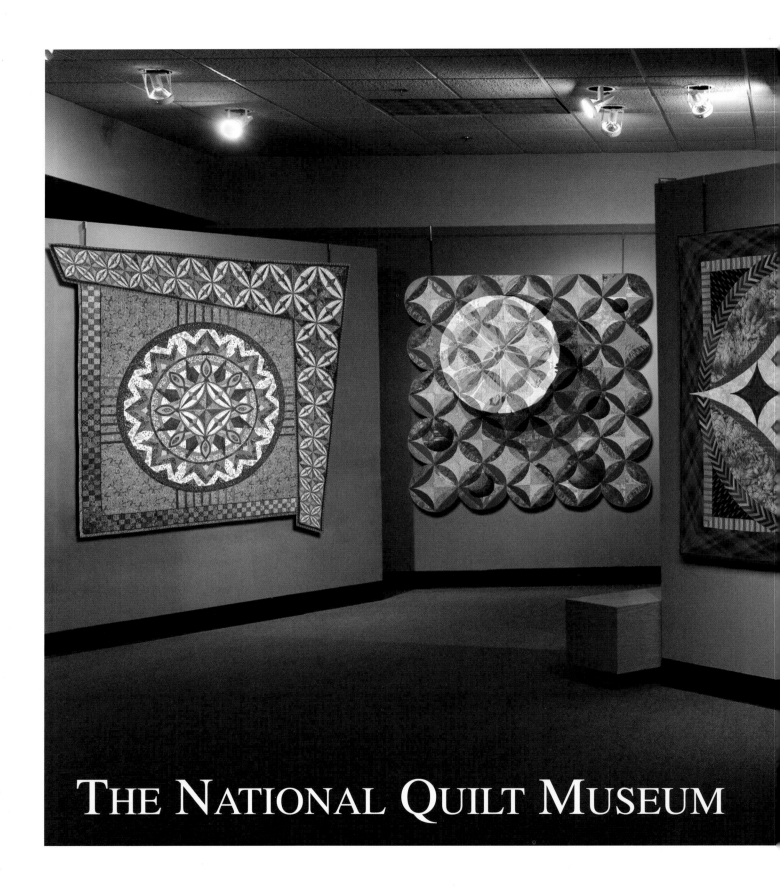

THE NATIONAL QUILT MUSEUM

The National Quilt Museum
215 Jefferson Street • Paducah • Kentucky 42001 • www.quiltmuseum.org • (270) 442-8856

First Place
Robin Gausebeck
Rockford, Illinois

Meet Robin

Much of my life has been spent dancing to a different drummer or, as Robert Frost put it in my favorite poem, following "the road less taken." My foray into quilting has been no different. With no history of quilting in my family and with parents whose tastes tended toward the decidedly modern rather than traditional, I have enjoyed exploring on my own and going where the fabrics and colors have led me.

Unfortunately, I often find that my quilt designs are a little too ambitious and it seems as though every quilt that I make calls for something that I don't yet know how to do. No matter—I just plunge in anyway. This keeps me on my toes, stretches my abilities, sometimes causes problems, but ultimately leads to a greater appreciation of the possible (and sometimes the impossible). When I look back over my seven years of quilting, I am amazed at how much I have grown.

As quilters go, I do not have a huge stash of fabrics, but even so there is much more than I could ever use up in a lifetime of quilting. My challenge is to find new ways to combine fabrics that on the surface don't speak to each other very well (multicolored hand-dyes and Asian prints or Paula Nadelstern prints and plaids, for example). Maybe I should take some more advice from Robert Frost—"good fences make good neighbors." I have no art training but I can throw a bunch of fabric onto my design wall with the best of them.

This is my fourth year as a finalist in the New Quilts from an Old Favorite contest, and I have loved the continuing challenge of taking a traditional block and making something new and fresh. The dichotomy of structure/no structure suits my admittedly quirky

way of designing a quilt almost literally. A quilt title will pop into my head and my task becomes how to give that title life and substance. This contest has also become rather an addiction for me. I already have a rough design for next year's theme, Baskets, but am still waiting for the Jacob's Ladder inspiration to strike. I am always amazed at how very different each of the finalist and winning quilts are from one another. Our personal journeys obviously lead us down very diverse creative paths.

There probably has been no greater thrill in my quilting life than turning a corner at The National Quilt Museum and seeing a quilt of mine hanging on the wall. I feel immensely proud to have something that I have created exhibited in such a remarkable space. My husband, Steve, is equally proud of what I do and has encouraged me every step of the way, even when I tell him nicely that, no, I can't go with him somewhere because I have to quilt.

Inspiration and Design

I'm not exactly sure where the inspiration for ORANGE BLOSSOM SPECIAL originated. Although the title came to me right away, I didn't want it to be too literal. I often enjoy brainstorming quilt ideas with my husband and we both agreed that building a quilt from variously sized and shaped blocks would have good visual interest as well as presenting me with a unique piecing challenge.

Electric Quilt® 6 software was a huge help, once I had a rough sketch of what I wanted. I spent many hours drafting variations and when I was done, I think I had about 75 unique versions to choose from. The Custom Set feature of EQ allowed me to place the blocks into

Orange Blossom Special 56½" x 56½"

I have no art training but I can throw a bunch of fabric onto my design wall with the best of them.

the body of the quilt one by one, not caring whether the corners of the quilt met in a regular fashion, only making sure that I ended up with a quilt center with straight outside edges.

I love playing with color and I decided to work with gradations of two color families—green and purple. I arranged them so that the green began with the brightest in the center and moved to dark to anchor the edges, and the purple worked in the opposite direction. A combination of hand-dyed and commercial cottons gave me the palette I needed. After auditioning a variety of fabrics I found an orange fabric whose visual texture actually resembled the rough peel of an orange. I am pleased that the finished quilt really stayed visually true to my original EQ design, with a kind of luminosity in the bright green at its heart.

Both the contrasting appliqué and the quilting motifs that echo the design in the focus blocks are a variation on a medieval design that I selected mainly because it fit the space well and was not visually distracting from the overall design. The green areas were all quilted in the traditional Orange Peel design, some sections extending into the border with the variegated thread I used in the body. This helped integrate the borders and the center and add visual interest. To achieve this step, I used EQ software to create a stencil. I printed an entire sheet of heavy card stock with ¾" diameter Orange Peel patterns. I stitched over every line with a jeans needle (no thread) to form a perforated stencil. I used a pounce pad to transfer the markings to the quilt.

To reinforce the focus blocks, I hand couched purple Superior Razzle Dazzle™ thread around all of the appliqués, a technique I learned in a class with Mariya Waters.

Technique
To be perfectly honest, I had real doubts about my ability to construct my Orange Peel blocks using conventional curved-piecing methods. I seriously feared that my blocks would not square up nicely and lie flat. So I built the blocks by stitching the various pieces—borders, arcs, and "peel"—to stabilizer that remained in the quilt. I chose Ricky Tims' Stable Stuff® Poly because I had used it before and already had a supply on hand.

Drafting my design in EQ enabled me to print each final block drawing onto the Stable Stuff, which works beautifully in my inkjet printer. I had previously numbered each block in the design, assigned a "style" number to each Orange Peel variation, and noted the orientation of each block in the quilt—as drawn; rotated 90, 180, or 270 degrees; or mirror-imaged.

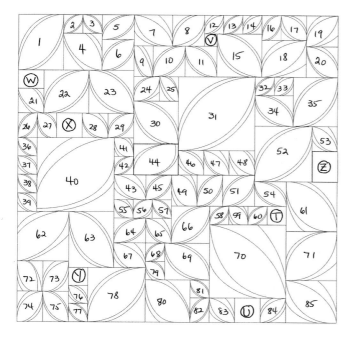

A Microsoft® Excel® spreadsheet was invaluable in the planning and construction process. For each individual block, I listed: (1) the block number, (2) the EQ block style number, (3) the height and width, (4) rotation (if any), (5) mirror-imaging (if any), and (6) which fabrics were selected for that block. Because only a couple of the 85 blocks were identical, this spreadsheet told me exactly how each foundation needed to be printed and how each block needed to be constructed. In addition, I was able to sort the data in the spreadsheet in various ways to make construction more efficient. I also used this data to calculate how large each of the appliqué and quilting motifs needed to be to fit properly into each block.

Working with the central part of each block first, I laid a piece of purple fabric right-side up on the right side of the Stable Stuff foundation, making sure that my piece of fabric completely covered that central area. This turned out to be a great way to use up irregularly shaped scraps. I pinned the fabric in place, turned the

piece to the back side, and stitched just outside what would have been the seam line on the block. The Stable Stuff was thin enough to allow me to see the outline from the back so I knew exactly where to sew. I trimmed the purple fabric so that I had approximately ¼" allowance beyond my stitching line.

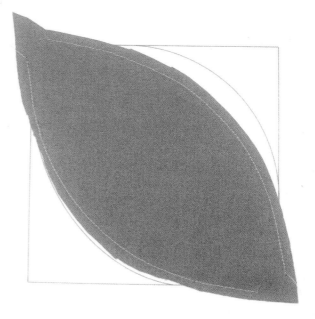

Next, I did the same thing with the green fabric, using a separate piece for each outside area, making sure that my grain lines were square to the edges of the block and that sufficient fabric extended over the sides of the block to allow for trimming the outside seam allowance to ¼". I then stitched these pieces to the Stable Stuff.

Using the same EQ block diagram, I printed just the reversed arc shapes onto freezer paper and used these as templates for the orange appliqué pieces. I cut the fabric around the templates a little longer than necessary at the ends so that there was an extra allowance for trimming. A paintbrush, a little spray starch, and a good stiletto helped me turn nice sharp curves. I removed the freezer paper and positioned each arc on the block, using a light box for accuracy. The appliqué piece now covered the raw edges of the green and purple fabrics and the initial stitching line. Using invisible thread and a very small zigzag stitch, I sewed the orange pieces to the foundation. I trimmed the entire block to the finished size plus ¼".

Once all of the blocks were completed and laid out on the design wall, I established a logical piecing sequence. This was a critical step since nearly all of the seams were partial seams and had to be sewn together in the proper order. Since the EQ block outline was printed on the reverse side of the Stable Stuff Poly, I was able to match printed line with printed line and achieve a perfectly square and dimensioned top.

The use of Stable Stuff had some advantages and disadvantages.

Advantages:

• I did not have to do any curved piecing.

• Stable Stuff becomes a soft collection of fibers once the quilt is washed so it can stay in the quilt.

• There is no paper to remove.

• The seam lines were printed on the foundation so sewing the blocks together was a breeze, despite all the partial seams.

Disadvantages:

• Because the Stable Stuff adds another layer, there were some bulky corners when the seams were sewn. I solved this problem by wetting, not washing, the finished top to slightly soften the Stable Stuff before adding the borders and layering the quilt.

• I found that in quilting the top, the presence of the Stable Stuff, albeit softer at that point, did not allow as much excess "puffiness" to be quilted out.

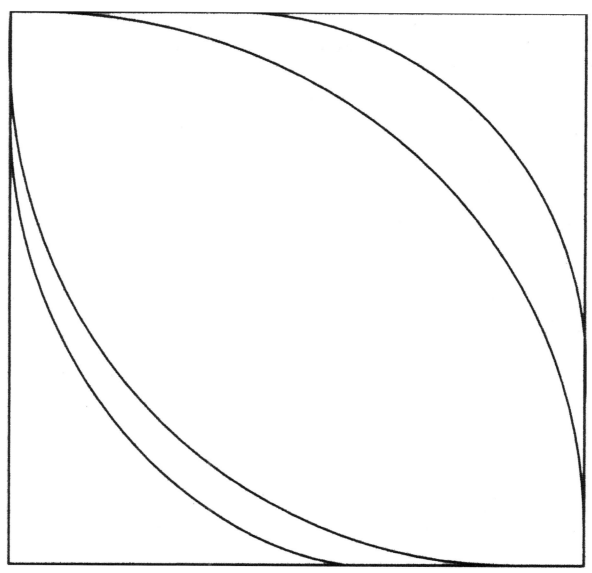

Block Foundation

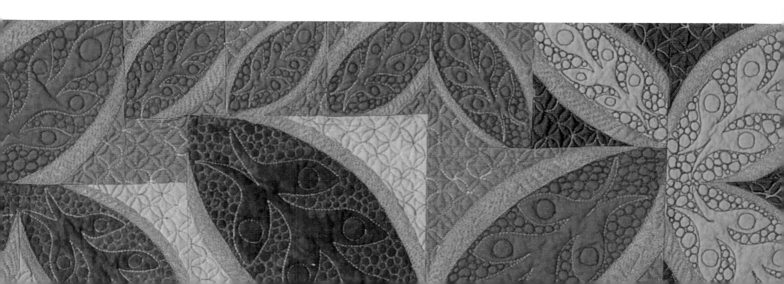

Photo by Mellisa Karlin Mahoney

Second Place
Sherri Bain Driver
Northglenn, Colorado

Meet Sherri

Several years ago, as a prizewinner at a guild show, I was asked to stand near my entry and chat with viewers who had come to see the quilts. One woman said to me, "Wow, you look just like a regular person!" I suppose she thought people who make cool quilts are magic and look different in some way. But I'm just a regular person who's especially passionate about making quilts. I devote lots of time and energy to designing and sewing them. Because my mother and grandmother were both accomplished seamstresses and I was always allowed to use scraps left from their projects, I learned to love fabric when I was very young. I started sewing my own clothes when I was eight years old, and was encouraged to deviate from printed patterns. When I started making quilts, I took the same approach.

My interest in quilting really took off in the late '80s when some friends organized a monthly guild and also a small quilting bee that met weekly. Both of those groups are still going strong. Inspired by the bee experience, I dipped my toe into the book business when a friend and I wrote a book about quilting bees. Another book and published patterns and articles followed, which led to my employment with several quilting magazines. I currently work as an editor for a quilt magazine, which helps keep me informed about new fabrics, products, techniques, and people. I enjoy helping others appreciate the beauty of quilts and the magic of their creation. I taught classes for many years and always thrill to the look on quilters' faces when they make their first quilt or master a new technique.

For many years I've been drawn to ikat fabrics. These fabrics have patterns or designs dyed into the yarns before the fabric is woven. The patterns can be as simple as a subtle color change along the warp or weft or extremely intricate motifs where patterns are dyed in both warp and weft yarns. I first discovered ikats in the 1980s and now have a large closet full of these unique beauties.

Inspiration and Design

SANDIA SUNSET was made specifically for this challenge. I love to design quilts, and I especially enjoy putting a new spin and my own personal stamp on a traditional design; the New Quilts from an Old Favorite contest is perfect for this approach. I look forward to it every year, even though I sometimes don't get a quilt finished in time to enter. I enjoy the design process and doodle design ideas in a graph-paper book. I bring this sketchbook on road trips and have been known to miss an entire state while buried in a page of ideas. I think I have as much fun before any needle touches fabric as I do after construction begins.

I draw inspiration for my quilts from everywhere, especially Native American arts, architecture, and nature. I don't try to duplicate an image, but instead use the interplay of light, color, texture, and shape to create a visual effect that hints at the original inspiration. I love color and fabric and creating something that is more than the sum of its pieces.

As I sketch a design, I don't worry about how to sew the project because I don't want my designs to be limited by my current technical abilities. I know that I'll eventually figure out how to construct anything I draw. I may spend weeks thinking about techniques for a particular design before I begin making a quilt. There are always several ways to sew anything, so I like to think

Sandia Sunset 58" x 58"

I enjoy helping others appreciate the beauty of quilts and the magic of their creation.

through all the construction steps, considering the pros and cons of different techniques, before I choose a method and get started in earnest. Once I get going, my quilts usually come together quite quickly.

SANDIA SUNSET began as a small graph-paper sketch. With the sketch in hand, I searched through favorite fabrics to assemble a group of ikats and woven stripes in colors that make my heart sing and reflect a range of values to highlight the various shapes. Light fabrics are always the hardest for me to pick, and I don't have lots of them in my stash because I don't find them as pretty or dramatic as many other fabrics. I know they are necessary, so I look for them every time I shop for fabric, just to be sure I always have some in my stash.

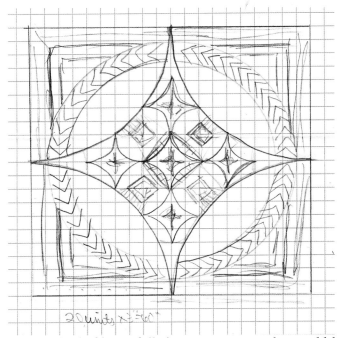

I enlarged the sketch, drafting a full-size paper pattern that could be cut along the drafted lines and ironed onto various fabrics. The fabric pieces were cut out, adding ¼" to edges of each paper piece and then sewn together. The chevron circle was created by cutting bias strips from a stripe, stitching them to the paper pattern, and pressing to reshape them into curves. The final quilt is very similar to my initial sketch; the only adjustment to my design was adding the dark curve that separates the peachy background of the inner Orange Peel shapes from the batik melon-shaped piece, because I didn't like these fabrics touching.

The colors in my quilt inspired the name. Sandia Peak in New Mexico turns these colors as the sun sets. *Sandia* is the Spanish word for watermelon.

Technique

Like most of my NQOF quilts, this one began as a simple sketch on graph paper. I considered the Orange Peel blocks printed on the entry form and fiddled with them with paper and pencil. I liked the curved square set on point to look more like a diamond than a square. Configuring five of them in the shape of a plus sign I could see that larger curves could surround the smaller five blocks.

Before starting a new design I often study photos of quilts that I consider my best. I think about which techniques have been successful in previous quilts, what didn't work well, and which design features I may want to revisit.

Many of my quilts have large circular motifs or centers, and that seemed ideal for an Orange Peel design. Reversing each quarter of the center circle created a curved, on-point diamond, a perfect start for an Orange Peel design. I drew smaller on-point diamonds inside the large one, and then started looking through my favorite ikats for a fabric to fussy-cut the smaller diamonds. Once that fabric was chosen, I looked for a lighter fabric for the background for the center area. I found a swirly peach and purple print, and also a small piece with a stripe. Although I didn't have much of the stripe, I like using a second light color to create a subtle secondary pattern.

From my stash I pulled several other compatible stripes and ikats and pinned them to my design wall to see how well they would play together and to see where they might work in the design. The narrow stripe was perfect to create a circle around the center, and when added to the sketch, I realized I could make the stripey circle go under the large on-point diamond to create a layered look. Now I was excited!

The smaller pieces in the quilt center were drafted on graph paper, plastic templates were made, and the center was assembled using traditional piecing. I cut oversized patches for the outside edges of this inner portion of the quilt, making it much larger all around than needed.

Keeping the same proportions as the graph-paper sketch, the design was redrawn full-size on Sulky® Totally Stable™ stabilizer, using Renae Haddadin's Amazing Rays® tool for the curves (much better than the yardstick compass I used in the past). Totally Stable is much more flexible than freezer paper and far easier to manipulate under the sewing machine. The Totally Stable was cut apart to serve as pattern pieces that I pressed onto the wrong sides of the appropriate fabrics. The center piece was carefully placed on the wrong side of the pieced center portion of the design and ironed in place. I crossed my fingers that I had placed it correctly and trimmed this pieced section ¼" beyond the edge of the paper pattern.

My tools: a large sheet of Sulky Totally Stable, calculator, pencil, measuring tape, and the Amazing Rays compass tool

Fussy-cutting ikat fabrics has become a hallmark of my style. Many quilters use mirrors to preview the kaleidoscopic effects formed by fussy-cutting, but I prefer to be surprised when I see what develops.

The fabric pieces were cut out, adding ¼" to edges of each paper piece, and then sewn together. The chevron circle was created by cutting bias strips from a stripe, stitching them to the paper pattern, and pressing to reshape them into curves. The final quilt is nearly identical to my initial sketch.

Photo by Mark J. Ferring

Third Place
Karen Watts
Houston, Texas

Meet Karen

This year I celebrated my 20th anniversary of quilting. I remember the date well because I went to Ohio to visit my grandmother in April 1991, and she took me to a shop that was half counted cross-stitch and half quilt shop. I was doing a lot of cross-stitch back then, but I'd always loved fabric, having grown up with a mother who sewed everything *EXCEPT* quilts! A good friend of mine had recently shown me a Log Cabin quilt she had started and I was intrigued. It was on that fateful trip to Ohio that a fat quarter packet in The Daisy Barrel caught my eye, and the rest is history. My first quilt was a sampler, made by using cardboard templates and scissors, and sewn on my mother's 1949 Singer® Featherweight. I finished the top, but before I quilted it I made about a dozen more, thus establishing my habit of having MANY projects going at the same time!

involved with a guild right away, and joined a bee that was just starting up. We still meet weekly, and celebrate our 14th anniversary in April 2011. One of my favorite things to do in the guild or bee is participate in challenges. Our guild entered the AQS Ultimate Guild Challenge three times and placed twice, and each time my quilt was one of the eight chosen to represent the guild. In 2007 we won first place with our challenge theme, Fruit. My STRAWBERRY FIELDS quilt is still one of my favorites. My Seasons theme quilt, MARINER, was inspired by a photo taken of my daughter at Girl Scout camp when she was 12.

STRAWBERRY FIELDS

My first quilt

Moving from Southern California to Houston in 1994 only added fuel to the fire. By chance I had landed in one of the two quilt capitals in the country! I got

MARINER

Tangerine Dream 55" x 55"

I had a lot of fun coming up with the different blocks and layouts and I may revisit this concept in the future.

This has been a whirlwind year! I started working on my Orange Peel design in late 2009 and began constructing the blocks in December. Usually I'm finishing my contest entry days before the deadline; this time I had the bright idea to finish my quilt in time to display it at our local guild show in May 2010. I'm really glad I did. TANGERINE DREAM took first place in its category, Innovative, and Best of Show! The deadline for entries for the IQA Houston show was about two weeks later, so I thought, "Why not?" I entered and was thrilled to be juried in and even more thrilled to win a third-place ribbon. What a great reward for finishing early.

As if that wasn't enough excitement for one year, our daughter graduated from high school and she and I went to France for two weeks. My husband and I moved our son to Albuquerque, moved our daughter to college, and broke ground on my new studio at our place in New Mexico. Our move from Houston to Cloudcroft, New Mexico, will take place sometime in 2011.

Inspiration and Design

The final version of my Orange Peel variation is very different from my first idea. My first thought was that the football shape in the block looked very organic, and I wanted to do something with vines and leaves, maybe in an Art Nouveau style. When I ran across a piece of fabric with surfboards all over it, the light bulb went off! My husband and I lived in Southern California before moving to Houston, and he was an avid surfer. Surfboards can be wonderful pieces of art, and the shape made me think of my Orange Peel blocks. I decided I could put many different designs in my Orange Peels and started drawing my ideas.

I started by drawing different pieced patterns, such as checkerboard, strips, and two different suns.

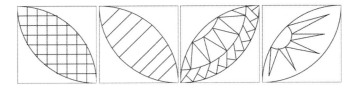

Then I tried clamshells, a flower, and a few more unusual designs.

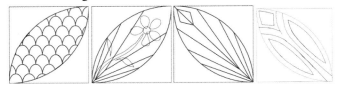

One of my favorites is the swirl, so that one ended up in the center. My last designs used my favorite dots.

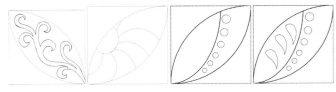

I auditioned many, many different layouts using various combinations of blocks. I wanted to use a variety of my block designs, but the quilt needed to have unity; I didn't want it to look like a hodgepodge of unrelated blocks!

I tried over four dozen different layouts.

For awhile I was determined to make some kind of checkerboards work. In the end I abandoned both the checkerboard Orange Peels and edge blocks. At this point I designed the Orange Peels with dots to use as border blocks, and finally replaced the checkerboard setting triangles with a special block I drew.

As I said, the Swirly block was one of my favorites, and some of my layouts used it in the center and the corners. But that made a total of 12 of those blocks, and after I made one of them I changed the design so I only had to make four. That block is fused, and the cutting out and stitching around it was very time-consuming. Four Swirly blocks would be just fine! I had a lot of fun coming up with the different blocks and layouts. The possibilities are endless and I may revisit this concept in the future.

Technique

I used many techniques in constructing my Orange Peel blocks. That's one of the reasons it was fun to make. If I got bored with one set of blocks, I could move on to a totally different technique. Some of my blocks were paper pieced. Since paper piecing can be difficult for some, I'd like to share some tips that I feel make it easier and discuss fabric painting.

Precut your fabric to the general shape of the finished piece, adding a generous seam allowance. I use ⅜" and just rough cut the pieces. This allows you to place them more accurately when sewing and also reduces fabric waste.

Use a tiny stitch when sewing your fabric to the paper, as it makes removing the paper much easier.

After sewing a piece to the paper, open the fabric and press it. Before adding the next fabric piece, fold back the paper on the next stitching line. You will see the seam allowance of the piece just sewn hanging over. Since you have cut generous-sized pieces, the seam allowance will be more than ¼". Trim it to ¼". Now you can easily line up the next piece with the trimmed edge without having to guess at the proper alignment.

If I am adding a light fabric to a dark one, I trim the seam allowance to slightly less than ¼", and make sure I completely cover the dark seam allowance with the light fabric piece. This eliminates shadowing on the front of the block.

In two of the different blocks I used a special fabric featuring my experimental painting. You may be familiar with the beautiful Skydyes™ painted fabric made and sold by Mickey Lawler. She also has a book explaining her process (see Resources, page 93). One day a group of friends and I decided to play around with that technique. We used Pebeo Setacolor® fabric paint, available at Dharma Trading Company (www.dharmatrading.com). This paint has a very soft hand when applied to fabric; it does not make the fabric stiff at all, behaving more like a dye. It can even be used on sheer fabrics, such as silk and organza.

Setacolor comes in transparent, opaque, and pearlescent colors. The transparent colors allow underlying colors to show through, and are best used on light-colored fabrics. The opaque and pearlescent colors give good coverage and can be used on dark fabrics as well as light. We used the transparent Setacolor and diluted it 1:1 with water. This made it very easy to work with and gave great color on our fabrics. We painted on white PFD (prepared for dying) cotton, plain muslin, and light colored batiks. The batiks are fun because the designs on the fabric can show through the paint.

Applying the paint can be done in many ways. Different sizes of paintbrushes will give different effects, but you can also use balled-up fabric or paper towel, stamps, or almost any other item you can put paint on! For one of my pieces I used a plastic fork. After I had painted different colors on the fabric I dipped the fork into pearlescent paint and dragged the tines across the fabric, making four skinny parallel lines.

Mixing colors is fun too. My favorite piece is the one I used in TANGERINE DREAM, and it looked like a beautiful sunset. I used yellow, red, and fuchsia paints, which made different shades of reds, oranges and pinks when combined, then added small swipes of blue here and there. After I was satisfied with the colors, I dipped a wad of muslin in the pearlescent paint and stamped it on, giving it a kind of a silvery cloud effect.

When you're through painting your fabrics, lay them flat and let them air dry. When dry, iron on the reverse side using the cotton setting for at least 5 minutes. This fixes the paint. After fixing, the colors resist machine washing at 100° F and dry cleaning.

Photo by Gerard Reuter

Fourth Place
Nancy Eisenhauer
Belleville, Illinois

Meet Nancy

I don't remember the first time I picked up a needle and thread. It seems I have always been around fabric and yarn. I own a Log Cabin quilt that was made by one of my great-grandmothers in 1885, and a crocheted bedspread made about 1937 by another great-grandmother. Needlecraft is surely in my genes. I remember going to my grandparents' farm as a child and looking at my grandmother's latest quilt. It would be ceremoniously unfolded and held by all those looking on. She made one quilt a year—pieced on her treadle sewing machine or hand appliquéd, and then hand quilted. The quilt frame was set up in the "front room" during the winter. The room had windows on three sides so there was a lot of good winter light. I'm sure it was also chilly in there. The only heat Grandma and Grandpa had were a couple of oil stoves in the kitchen and TV room. As I grew up I thought that quilting must be very hard. Look how long it took Grandma to make a quilt!

Through my growing-up years, I made clothes for my dolls and then myself. After college, life got really busy: I started teaching and had a family. My sewing machine was relegated to repairs and the occasional home-dec project. When I retired from teaching elementary school in 2006, I returned to my sewing machine, but not to garment sewing. My interest in quilting had been awakened by friends and my sister-in-law, Gail Warning. I bought a kit but the quilt I made from it didn't provide the satisfaction I craved. I remember Gail asking me if I thought I was more interested in making traditional quilts or art quilts. Having just finished a traditional quilt with blocks and more blocks, all the same pattern, I said, "Art quilts." I have never looked back.

I love manipulating fabrics, thread, paints, and whatever else I can find to create a mood or memory. My camera is one of my favorite tools for capturing inspiration. I have a box full of prints of everything from tiny flowers to huge bridges. There are enough quilt ideas in there to last two lifetimes! I think all of us have an urge to be creative with something. It may be cooking, gardening, or even organizing. The trick is to find a way to channel your creativity and then go for it.

Inspiration and Design

As I thought about this year's contest theme, I looked at Orange Peel blocks from several sources to see what variations there might be on the block. As I was considering what I could do with those elliptical shapes, my mind was also playing with the word "orange." What if I made an orange Orange Peel? What if the peels floated all over? What if I put oranges on it? How would I do that? What about orange slices? I was off and running.

I took a design class at The National Quilt Museum taught by Katie Pasquini Masopust in September 2009. It was an awesome experience. If you ever get the chance to take a class at the museum, don't pass it up. We experimented with abstract forms and then added color. We learned a lot about color selection and especially the use of color value. This gave me the knowledge I needed to make an all-orange quilt work.

I started with one of the Orange Peel blocks from Electric Quilt software. That would be my background. I decided that the light source for the quilt would be in the upper left corner. That gave me the shading for the blocks. What if I superimposed an orange slice on

Oranges 58" x 58"

Don't give up on an idea for a quilt just because you can't use your favorite method.

the background? I took an orange, sliced it in half, put paint on it, and started printing and discovered that real slices aren't symmetrical. From the best print, I traced the orange slice onto acetate and placed it on the block background. I added shading and some oranges floating around it.

To make the slice stand out, I used a ghost-layering technique, also from Katie. All the shapes within the slice are two values lighter than the rest of the quilt. By adding the two rings of shadow, the contrast was heightened even more. I used 107 different fabrics in the quilt, not all of them "right-side up."

The Orange Peel quilt cried out for a scalloped edge. I simply used the curve of the peel for the edges, except along the top. Piping along a knife-edge finished it off nicely.

Technique

When I looked at my full-scale drawing of ORANGES, I paused. There were so many small pieces, especially in the orange slice, that I questioned whether I could indeed render my idea in fabric. In the design, there are both straight and curved seams. Piecing or appliqué?

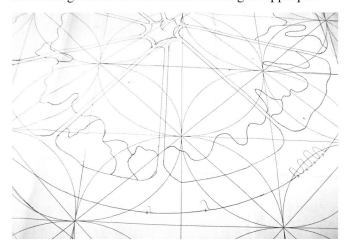

I decided that I would do some piecing on the straight seams and machine appliqué the rest. I made strip-sets of two fabrics that I used for the orange peel in each block. That way I got a nice straight seam down the middle of each peel. I traced the outline of the peel on the strip and cut it out, adding ¼". I turned the edges under with starch and pressed them over the poster board pattern piece to get the edges just right. I also pieced the scooped-out edge pieces of the block that meet in the corners. All pieces were machine appliquéd after edges were either turned or tucked under another piece. Again, I followed Katie's technique.

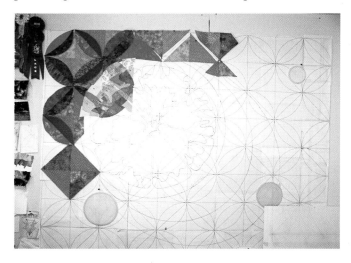

Adding fabrics to the master pattern

On my drawing I numbered the pieces from 1 to 7 to indicate the value of the fabric to be used. My fabrics were laid on the floor in matching value groups. I had a second copy of the drawing affixed to poster board that I cut up for pattern pieces. A third copy of the drawing was traced onto Sulky Totally Stable fusible stabilizer. I fused all the pressed pieces to the stabilizer until I could zigzag stitch around all edges with monofilament thread to secure them, working a small section at a time. I assembled the top in three long sections and joined them after completion.

I put off quilting the top for a few weeks until I decided how to quilt it. I knew that the orange slice would be quilted to look like a natural orange. The rest took some time to figure out. After experimenting with some extra fabric, I decided to use one motif on the background of each block and simple echo quilting on the peels. I didn't want to bind

the edge of the quilt. I had used knife-edges before, but I decided to add piping to it this time. By programming a series of straight stitches and zigzags into my machine, I was able to add thread "stripes" to the piping before machine sewing it to the quilt top. The meeting points of the piping were hand sewn from the front and back. I finished by turning under the backing and sewing it to the back of the piping.

This quilt forced me to use several tools in my technique toolbox. I like to take technique classes and I found that even if I'm not crazy about a certain technique, it might be the one that works best for a given quilt. Don't give up on an idea for a quilt just because you can't use your favorite method. Try something new.

Photo by Christopher Weston

Fifth Place
Michael Michalski

Brooklyn, New York

Meet Michael

I've been a fan of the New Quilts from an Old Favorite contest since its inception in 1994. I began paying serious attention to quilts in the early 1990s. Most seemed to fall into two categories—traditional designs and pictorial art quilts. The NQOF books showed me there was a middle ground, that there were no boundaries on what you could represent. I had the freedom to play, giving my artistic side free rein, while still staying with the geometry that satisfied my scientific background. AQS, along with artists such as Michael James and Nancy Crow, pointed me in a direction that has become an all-encompassing passion. I now challenge myself that if I can draw it I will find a way to make it.

My pathway to quilting is probably one shared by many. I taught myself how to sew as a teenager. Making clothes was a way to show I wasn't going to be like everyone else. This came in handy a decade later when I decided to leave the world of the chemistry laboratory for theatrical costume making. I used my leisure time to do home decorating projects for myself and others, which was a welcome relief from trying to make things that would fit a human body.

My first quilt was intended for my mother. I visited all the little odds and ends fabric stores prevalent at that time (how I miss them) and bought a collection of calicoes and shirtings in navy, brown, and beige. I chose to feature a Lone Star set on point in a background of Log Cabin blocks. Why should one start with a quick and easy project? Since some of the fabrics were light in weight, and to facilitate the use of non-cotton fibers, I lined each diamond or strip individually with a coordinating solid as I pieced it in. I decided to hand quilt the center, tie the cabins, and machine quilt the border—a veritable quilting sampler!

A coworker was moving and she gave me her quilting frame that became the main decorating feature of my living room for most of a year. As my mother lived in the snow belt of upstate New York, I used a double layer of high-loft batting. I think it would have been warm enough for the Arctic. After the chore of stitching through that I didn't try hand quilting again for years. It is still a UFO, waiting for me to remove the hand quilting from the half that is done so I can make it practical.

While I was pushing my way (literally) through that first quilt, I visited a quilt show at Pier 92 (which turned out to be the last major quilt show in NYC, another institution sorely missed). There I was introduced to the wonders of fabric and tools made just for quilting, and saw that quilts could be more than just bed coverings. Now I am living the quilt life full time. I find my time torn between commissions, contests, teaching (spreading the joy), and group projects. I spearhead my union's yearly raffle quilt, and the newly formed guild, Broadway Gentlemen's Quilt Auxiliary, has set a goal of an annual donation quilt. It's great that I get to work with so many crafty people. I find time is rare for making things for myself. I am happy to say days full of design and fabric play suit me just fine.

Design *(The Evolution of an Idea)*

Design is my favorite aspect of the process. I outline a basic idea and work on it for months until I feel I'm ready to stop fussing. Until a few years ago, I'd do my sketches on graph paper with colored pencils. Each

Cosmic Plum 70½" x 70½"

The tried-and-true methods have had years to get the problems worked out of them— reinventing the wheel takes time.

change entailed restarting the drawing from scratch. Now with computers in the picture (I could no longer work without EQ!), it is so easy to make alterations yet the designing takes even longer. I can draw a multitude of variations and don't want to stop until the ideas do. It is well known that "it's not a quilt until it's quilted," but it's also not a quilt unless it leaves the drawing board and is made in fabric.

Once I have a drawing I like, I choose one or two fabrics I really like and base the color scheme on them, even though they often end up not being in the quilt. I buy more fabrics than I need, spread them all over the floor, and pull out those that don't work for me. I use what remains to color the design. I am happier when I closely match what I have drawn instead of trying new things as I am doing the construction. I am not one to let the design evolve as it is being sewn. It works better if I can see it before I make it. I find that if I do make changes I usually end up spending time ripping them out and going back to the original plan. This quilt was a challenge for me in that I never finalized a plan before I needed to get the sewing underway. This proved to be a problem later. I've learned it doesn't work for me to move forward in the process until my design tells me it's ready.

I'd thought about entering the NQOF contest for some time and felt Orange Peel was finally the challenge for me. I blocked out my year's time to allow three months for the construction, leaving me nine months to work out the design in my spare time. The traditional Orange Peel block has large spaces between arcs, so I reset the peels in an interlocking pattern, using Compass Stars to fill the shape, and put spinning Log Cabins in the new spaces between. Add a more traditionally set border, color it orange and green, and I was done in two days!

That left me far too much time to think about it. At the time I was taking a class in designing with circles and curves at City Quilter (how well timed), and the instructor, Judy Doenias, suggested I could give it punch by using a value gradation. I thought why not vary the size and hue as well, and the skewed border was born.

Now the center needed a makeover to keep to the new style, and it reminded me of a flying saucer so I christened it Cosmic Plum.

Upon further reflection, it still didn't have that feel of a piece of modern art I was going for. It had become an exercise in perspective. I am known for having flanges in all my work. Lately I've been fond of adding squares and triangles as one does in quick-piece Cathedral Window frames. Why not try that with the stars? Thus the folded fabric Compass Star was born. It was finally time to begin sewing.

Technique
(How to Get from Drawing to Fabric)

I began constructing the skewed border, thinking it would be the most difficult section. (Little did I know the challenges awaiting me in the center.) The background was paper-foundation pieced. Templates were made for each star point, background section, and complete Orange Peel—255 templates in all. Making the borders mirror images at least allowed for doubling up in the cutting. Making Orange Peel/Compass Star blocks was a time-consuming yet satisfying task.

Each block was trimmed to size and the binding seamline marked. I chose to finish each as a separate unit, thinking that would make them stand out as well as

making it easier to get the tapered outline I sought. They were basted to the background, to be held in place later with the quilting. I also chose to bind the entire border before attaching it, as I thought of the quilt as a combination of three standalone pieces. The binding for the top and right edges of the entire quilt was basted behind the border so that it could come out from underneath it. This turned out to be a particularly tricky part; it would not lie flat and wanted to pull the slanted edges into square. Though I love the look of it, it is not something I would try again soon. The tried-and-true methods have had years to get the problems worked out of them—reinventing the wheel takes time.

The checked border was my favorite section. Finding and arranging all those purple and green fabrics was just my kind of project. It went together like a dream, probably because it was where I used the most traditional piecing. The green edge was a late addition to make the checkerboard stand out, where before it didn't hold its own. The facing came off and a quilted strip was added, a technique used in the hems of fancy gowns. My garment training comes into use every now and then!

Finally time to tackle the center! I started with a paper-pieced foundation, then inserted additional strips and triangles here and there. The Orange Peel was repeated as negative space in the outer ring. I made a round of peels reminiscent of peacock feathers. I found this big compass easy to construct…the first time. In trying to pull all the colors from the border, there was too much competition among them, so some of the patches were replaced (some more than once). Eventually I felt I had it tamed. I attached the two border sections, using a full-size drawing as a guide. The sections were united; maybe I had a shot at finishing it by the deadline.

Quilting is usually not one of my favorite tasks, but for this project I had so many ideas I was racing to get them on the fabric. I used a combination of in-the-ditch quilting, double outlining, and stippling, as well as motifs consisting of orange peels arranged both in radial wheels, like flowers, and linearly, like cables. I hope from now on the quilting portion will continue to be this much fun.

Making the Folded Fabric Compass Star

Each of these original blocks consists of four star points and four background pieces.

The templates for the points are made by adding half the width of the point to each long side for a turn back, then adding the seam allowance. I punched holes in the templates to mark the ends of the seams.

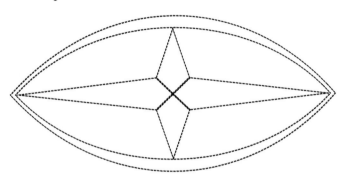

The four points are stitched together only where their faces meet (about ¾"). Press the seams open and trim the center to remove bulk.

Baste batting in place.

Fold a long star point (purple) in half lengthwise, wrong sides together, and sew between two of the background patches. Repeat with the opposite long point.

Fold the short points (green) and insert between the corresponding sides of the background. Trim the overlapping seam allowances at the center.

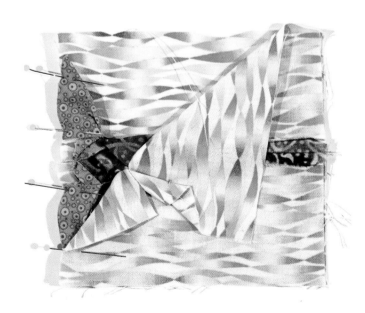

Steam press the seams open, taking care not to crease the star (I used a pressing ham), then turn the block over and steam the star. Use bamboo kebob skewers inserted in the narrow points to coax them into shape. If you didn't quilt the points, use forceps to push fiberfill in between the layers at the center, then tack along the center seams to hold it in place and give definition.

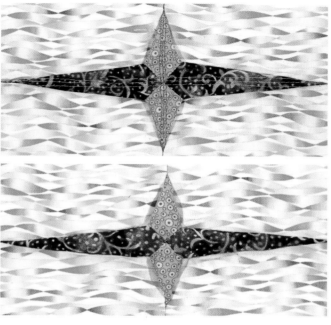

Quilted (top) and stuffed (bottom) Compass Star points

I wonder what other shapes can be made using this technique? I'm sure exploration could lead to something delightful, though at this point I'm on to something new!

Finalist
Mae Adkins
Casa Grande, Arizona

Meet Mae

I can't remember a time that I wasn't sewing in one form or another. My grandmother, Mae Strode, taught me how to sew around the age of five. My older sister, Carol, and I spent a lot of time in the summer at our grandparents' farm. Grandma would so patiently cut squares and let us sew them together. There was never a time she didn't have a quilt in progress or on the quilting frame. We used a lot of feed sacks to make our play clothes and cut up the scraps for the quilts. Carol is still partial to reproduction '30s' feed sack fabric, but not me.

Carol took me to my first AQS quilt show in Paducah seven years ago and I was amazed at the beautiful designs. It was the first time I had ever seen or heard of machine quilting. I was strictly a hand quilter up to that point but was never really good at it. Although I'd make several quilts tops through the year, only one would get completely finished.

The first step to becoming a machine quilter was my husband, Doug, buying me a tabletop frame for my domestic machine. I now have a Nolting® stitch-regulated machine with a heavy-duty freestanding frame. It was the best investment that I could afford and I've been very pleased.

Sharon Schamber has probably had the most influence on my quilting style and ability. Appliqué quilts are my favorite to make and I like Sharon's foundation glue-baste construction method the best. I never thought I would do fusible appliqué, but learned the hard way on this quilt there are times when it is necessary to get the look you want.

I started entering local judged quilt shows in Ohio. I found judges' comments are the best way to improve my quilting techniques. Getting blue ribbons in the local and state fairs was a real morale builder. In 2008 I won the Best of Show award at our local fair and was thrilled. Three years in a row I took the Peoples' Choice award at the Northwest Ohio Quilt Guild show. In 2008 at the urging of a dear friend, quilt teacher, and judge, Betty Fiser, I entered the museum's Burgoyne Surrounded contest. To my total amazement, my quilt THIRTEEN COLONIES—STARS OF THE REVOLUTION was chosen as one of the eighteen finalists. You can't imagine how I felt to have my quilt exhibited with all the beautiful, famous quilts at the museum.

After retiring in 2009, my husband and I moved to Arizona. I joined the Tucson Quilt Guild and the Arizona Quilters Guild. I was intimidated by the amazing quilters in Arizona. This was not in the league of county fair quilters. I decided to enter three quilts in the Tucson quilt show to get the judges reaction to my quilts. My machine-quilted entries both won blue ribbons, and the one I hand quilted won an honorable mention. The guild also selected my machine-embroidered appliqué with its square knot corded binding to receive the Arizona Quilters Hall of Fame award. The same quilt also received the Viewer's Choice honorable mention award. At the Phoenix Quilt Show two of my other quilts took second and third place. Needless to say my confidence in my quilting got a real boost.

I'm my own worst critic when it comes to meeting my quilting goals. I certainly have a lot to learn yet, and for the life of me I just can't make myself understand the color wheel. Maybe that is a good thing because most of the judges' good comments have to do with my choice of fabrics and color. I'm really looking forward to designing more quilts and improving my machine quilting. Someday I hope to own a larger computerized longarm to combine with my free-motion quilting.

Center design based on the Fiesta fabric collection from Elizabeth's Studio

*There comes a time when common sense
should take over and new ideas replace the tried
and true—the best lesson learned on my quilt.*

Inspiration and Design

The inspiration for my design was actually a French stained glass church window I saw on the Internet in 2009 while searching for a Frank Lloyd Wright® Collection window design for the fall Arizona Quilters Guild challenge called "The Wright Stuff."

I saved the picture to my computer and later printed it out and put it on my design wall for inspiration. It turned out that was a good thing, because my computer crashed in 2010 and lost everything. The original design had 12 medallions all surrounded by a diamond-shaped lattice-work with a small border.

One day while in the local quilt shop, I saw a Southwest design fabric that had a flowered circle as one of the many designs in the fabric. I bought a quarter yard and added it to my design wall. When the summer weather got too hot to spend much time outside, I thought that replacing the diamonds in the background with the Orange Peel block would be perfect for the challenge. I decided on one center medallion and added enough background and borders to meet the dimension requirements. The quilt evolved around this idea with quite a few design challenges and changes.

I have been doing real stained glass work for the last twenty years and my favorite glass is the opaque Spectrum™ opalescent glass. The colors are always there whether you have a light source or not. I have always loved the rich colors and textures of Maywood Studio's Shadow Play fabric, and the 3 Dudes Quilting shop in Phoenix carries every color in the line. I had made a sample of what I thought I wanted the color to be to take with me but replaced some after seeing the many choices.

After picking out the fabric, I had to get my design for the center onto the design board. I took a clear piece of template plastic and traced the circle design of my Southwest fabric and put that design in my overhead projector. I made a 31½" circle with a yardstick compass and centered my design over the circle and traced the design. I had to do some redrawing in the next step to get it centered within my circle.

My first attempt at the background Orange Peel was a 3" pieced block using EQ 6 for my pattern. After getting it all pieced and putting bias tape around it, I thought all the seams and the bias tape crossing was going to be a real quilting challenge—just too much bulk. Another problem I faced was that I wanted to put a crystal at every biased crossing and couldn't find any big enough to create the look I wanted. My background stayed on the design board for six weeks while I tried to decide whether to give up or start all over.

Since this was the first time I'd tried using bias tape, I also ran into problems with my center medallion but decided it was really the only method to use. I took down my pieced background, cut a wholecloth blue background, made a see-through template for the placement of my "football," and started all over again with a 2" grid. I liked the proportion a lot better in relation to the size of the quilt and crystals I wanted to use.

This quilt was a real learning experience. Its design just kind of evolved from one step to the next. The gold border around my medallion was lacking, so I decided to add the black circles. This contrasting border set the color design for the rest of the borders.

I think sometime in the future I would still like to do twelve medallions and expand the design. I've had several quilters ask if I was going to make the pattern for sale. I really like the colors and the black and gold border on the quilt. If I were to do it all over I would definitely use fusible appliqué and not feel like I was cheating. There comes a time when common sense should take over and new ideas replace the tried and true—the best lesson learned on my quilt.

Technique

STAINED GLASS APPEAL was a test of trial and error and I learned a lot from the process. I have never been good at drawing, so right from the start finding the right center for my quilt was my biggest challenge. After finding the fabric with the perfect design for the medallion, getting it from a 2" circle to 31½" was the next step. I ironed pieces of freezer paper together to make a big enough background for my circle. Using an overhead projector I was able to make my design any size I wanted. Because I was tracing the design from fabric onto template plastic it was a little distorted, so I divided my circle into quarters, refined one quarter of the drawing, and retraced that area on all four quarters of my circle.

The next step was to measure the quilt sides to determine what size to make the next border and come up with a design to fit the measurement. I was so pleased with the black circles on the gold border that I knew I wanted to use that color combination. I made the blocks by using smaller gold squares and adding oversized black squares to all four sides so the gold squares would be completely surrounded by black. After measuring this border I made a pattern for half of the next flowered fused border and added it to my quilt. The last border was made as a combination of the circle and squared borders to pull the design altogether.

The quilt has a 3" bias binding because I had originally thought of putting a looped corded binding to match the shape of the flowers around the outside to look like metal filigree. After doing a few loops and testing it on the quilt, I decided it was too fragile in comparison to the boldness of the quilt design.

I thought I would use a black cotton batting to avoid any bearding problems in quilting but it dulled the light blue center, so I used a white medium-weight Quilters Dream Poly batting to eliminate that problem. I did simple outline quilting in the appliquéd areas, small stippling in the background to make the design pop, and small teardrops in the black borders.

Photo by Sara Tate

Finalist
Elaine Braun
Paducah, Kentucky

Meet Elaine

Over the years, I have enjoyed learning crafts that include making stained glass windows, weaving authentic Alaska spruce root and cedar baskets, designing and stitching antique needlework samplers, and quilting. My first needlework competition was in 1990, when I entered my original sampler for the Good Housekeeping "Samplers for Literacy" campaign spearheaded by First Lady Barbara Bush. There were over a thousand entries and mine, along with 11 others, was featured in the *Good Housekeeping* magazine. I also entered an original sampler in the first AQS needlework competition in Nashville in 2007 where I took home the blue ribbon.

I started quilting about 13 years ago while living in Juneau, Alaska, mostly as a way to meet and enjoy the company of other quilters passing the long dark winter hours. In 1998, I invented and patented my material circle cutter. I also established my company Polar Notions. After a couple of years and stacks of fabric later, it occurred to me that quilters needed a way to organize their fabric after they got it home. We all love going into quilt stores, and, with that in mind, I designed an acid-free smaller version of the bolts that are used in stores. I then started the long process of acquiring my patent and searching for a manufacturer.

I was lucky enough to find a wonderful company in Texas to take on my dream. The mini-bolts caught on so well that when my husband and I retired, we moved to Paducah to be closer to the heart of quilting. Our lives revolve, for the most part, around quilting. We are vendors at all of the AQS sponsored shows as well as at the Houston Quilt Festival every year where we are able to meet our customers, new and old, and enjoy the talent of so many quilters.

I am a volunteer at The National Quilt Museum in Paducah where some of the best quilts in the world can be seen. I used to be intimidated, but now realize these same quilters started at the beginning, just like me, and now I am inspired by their talents. I took a class from George Siciliano in 2009 and fell in love with miniatures and the process he taught. My small quilt FIRE FLIES is in the museum's miniature collection. I was also a finalist in the 2010 AQS Quilt Show & Contest—Paducah with my miniature TROPICAL PLEASURES.

Technique

I learned of the New Quilts from an Old Favorite contest through my association with the museum. Because I have always loved the Orange Peel block, I decided to give this contest a try. I used my EQ6 software to create my templates for the Orange Peel blocks. The large Orange Peel blocks are 6" finished, as are the Framed Nine-Patch blocks. The small Orange Peel blocks are 3" finished, so four together form a 6" finished block.

It was then a process of deciding how to place the blocks and use different colors of fabric through a lot of trial and error. This is where the EQ6 program made the process easier. The pieces were constructed by strip piecing using ¼" seams.

When finished with the top I felt this quilt deserved better quilting than I would bring to it, so I asked Sally Terry, an accomplished, professional longarm quilter, to do the quilting. I truly enjoyed the process and am honored that this quilt was chosen as a finalist.

**When my husband and I retired, we moved
to Paducah to be closer to the heart of quilting.**

Framed Nine Patch

Key Block (41/100 actual size)

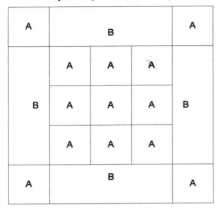

Cutting Diagrams

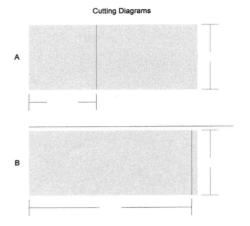

Framed Nine Patch

Key Block (29/50 actual size)

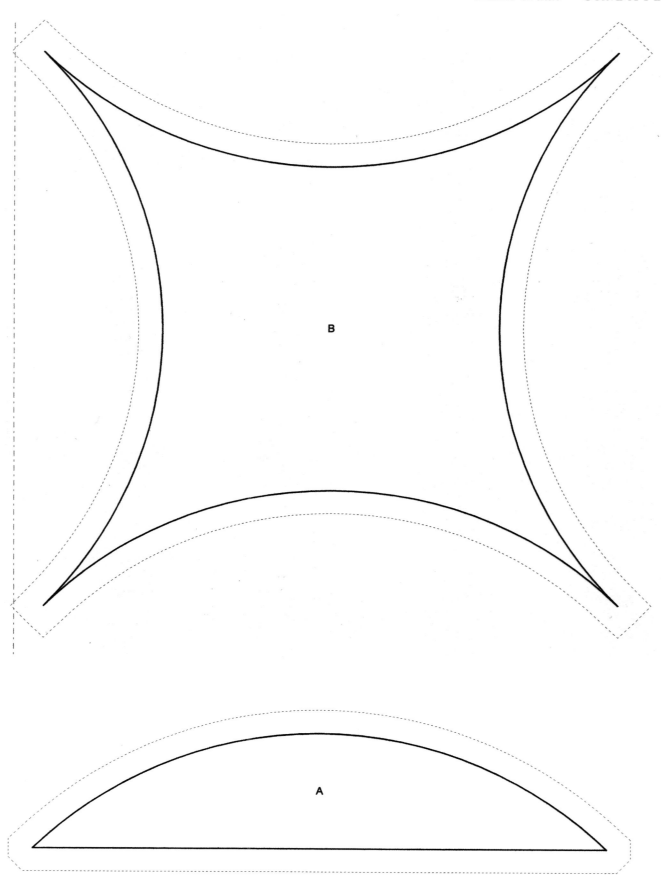

Photo by Jessica Pantoja

Finalist
Diane Kay Evans
Forest Ranch, California

Meet Diane

I started my first quilt in 1977. I had a homemade card-board triangle, fabric scraps from clothes making, old cut-up muslin curtains, and a new boyfriend. I wanted to impress him with my domesticity. The final stab-stitch quilting (through two layers of poly batt!) didn't happen until 1983, when our daughter was two years old. I'm pretty sure he didn't marry me because I was a quilter.

The world of quilting really opened up for me about a dozen years ago when I joined the Annie's Star Quilt Guild in Chico, California. I can't stress enough how great belonging to a guild is. Beginners should never hesitate to join. Access to the quilt books library, being with other quilters, and attending workshops with world-renowned quiltmakers really helped me grow. One workshop was with Karen K. Stone, designer of the first "peel" I ever made (see Resources, page 93).

Going to quilt shows and exhibits opened my eyes even further. My mom is ever the teacher and always on the lookout for something of interest to her four daughters. I have to thank her and my dad, Laura and Don Mac-Gregor, for taking me to the Nevada Museum of Art in Reno and introducing me to the quilts from Gee's Bend. Those quilts are so refreshing and appealing. Their makers created beauty out of "making do." It was quite an "ah-ha" moment when I realized that the dye-resist technique I thought I was looking at was really the deeper blue next to the faded denim of some overalls from which the pockets had been carefully removed.

I also have to thank my mom for making sure I got a sewing machine when I was 12, despite the fact that she had absolutely no skill or interest in handwork her-

self. And thanks to my dad for sharing my interest in fabric dyeing (although I have to say my heart skipped a beat when he called midmorning one day and said, "I'm dyeing").

John, my husband of 31 years, and I live in the Sierra Nevada foothills in northern California in the same house where we raised our four children. We hope to put the finishing touches on my sewing studio over a detached garage this summer. In addition to my passion for quilting, I've had a long-term interest in yoga (since my teens) and after a lifetime of more off than on again practice, I've been attending classes regularly for the past seven years. Like quilting, I know it's something I can do for the rest of my life and continue to grow in and enjoy.

Design and Inspiration

Something in me really responded to the Gee's Bend influence of making a quilt pattern-free. Challenges and contests always get my imagination rolling. When I read of the New Quilts from an Old Favorite contest, I really wasn't looking to enter anything, but my mind's eye popped open an idea for using the Orange Peel theme.

The next day I tried cutting a peel and appliquéing some spikes into it. It was frustrating, hard, and a fail-ure. But the idea persisted and I tried again from anoth-er angle. By hand basting the arc and cutting the spikes on the other side, I found I could make a freehand peel with some ease. I made 176 of them. I used my hand span to measure the final length and basted under the raw edges to finish the blocks to that size. Cutting and sewing them into 88 pairs was a lot more fun than try-ing to put them all together!

Hola Mola 64" x 64"

I have to thank Mom and Dad for introducing me to the quilts from Gee's Bend.

Technique

The peels were constructed by freehand cutting a rectangle slightly wider than my hand span and with a height greater than the length of my index finger.

*Layer and cut
2 colors*

I layered two colors together, folded the rectangle in half, and cut an arc to the tip of my index finger starting with an approximate ¼" at the edge.

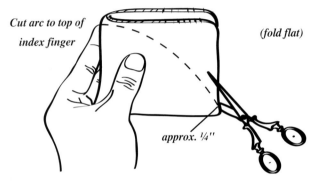

*Cut arc to top of
index finger*

(fold flat)

approx. ¼"

I basted the curved edge, clipped in seven deep triangles, and appliquéd them by hand. I stitched together the crescents and basted under the outer edges so the final measurement of the peel was the width of my hand span.

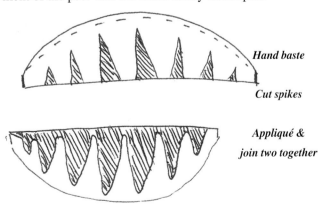

Hand baste

Cut spikes

*Appliqué &
join two together*

I used the old technique of hand to nose to measure the background, cutting twice the length. I joined (by hand) another two lengths and did a diagonal fold to make a square by cutting off the excess fabric. I used a long straight edge to lay out my first peels to establish the pattern. Arranging the blocks was actually one of the most trying

parts. They all got basted down but I did it in sections, not all at once.

I do have to say that having a deadline kept me on track and forced me to figure out problems as they arose. I spent many hours (days, actually) on my original concept for the middle, but when I tried it out, it was wrong. The clock was ticking. I had to come up with another idea *now*!

A couple of years ago I did a reproduction of the Rockefeller quilt (see Resources, page 93). I did that quilt primarily as reverse appliqué, so when I started mulling over a new center design, the Mola style idea started forming.

The true Molas from Central America start with many layers of fabric and each is cut away and stitched to reveal the color beneath. I changed the approach and basted an underlying color before I cut away to the top fabric to reverse appliqué.

I underlaid the turquoise and basted it in place before cutting away the red center. The same was done for the blue. The red center I had cut away, I folded in eighths, took a deep breath, and cut a half-peel on the fold. I used the same underlaying reverse-appliqué technique, then cut out the smaller "peels" and the center. After it was completed, I put it under the top and basted it in place before cutting away the excess blue.

Since everything else on the quilt was done machine- and measurement-free, I hand sewed the backing seam and scissor cut and hand sewed all the binding. Because there is so much dimension in the peels, I neither wanted (nor could do) very tight hand quilting. I chose to echo quilt the pattern from the center out.

The only thing I measured was the 4" sleeve for the back and to check the final measurements. The quilt is exactly my height—5' 4"

I have always believed that God creates in us an enthusiasm to start on journeys we are meant to take. That excitement got me started, but it was faith that got me through. I often had to think back to that original excitement as the "work" progressed, but I never tired of looking at the interplay of colors. I hope that when you view my quilt, it makes you happy.

Finalist

Ann Feitelson
Montague, Massachusetts

Ronna Erickson
Amherst, Massachusetts

Photo by Neil Erickson

Meet Ann

I always loved to do needlecrafts with my mother as a child. Thinking I was doing something unrelated, I went to art school and got an MFA in painting and an MA in art history. I was serious about being a painter for about 10 years; knitting and sewing were on back burners. I painted landscapes and still lifes set on striped tablecloths, and taught painting at several colleges. But I burned out on making a professional career of my personal perceptions and feelings. I went back to enjoying the crafts I had done with my mother and came to take them more seriously. I still love working with textiles. In some ways, 30 years later, I'm still involved with the subjects I loved when I was painting—I'm awed by the beauty of nature and want to capture it, I love working with stripes.

For a while, between painting and quilting, I was a serious knitter and wrote *The Art of Fair Isle Knitting.* Knitting sometimes features stripes, too! I work part-time at a yarn store and write freelance articles on the arts for a local newspaper.

I have been quilting for about 11 years. This is the sixth time I have been a finalist in the NQOF contest. It's nice when the chosen block coincides with something I've already been thinking about. This year's contest gave me an opportunity to work with a theme I'd already been working on—leaf quilts made exclusively with stripes, where stripes give the illusion of veins that diverge from the center of a leaf. I love leaves because they are a universal motif having to do with growth and nature. Stripes are always dynamic and exciting.

Meet Ronna

I have always enjoyed creating and making all sorts of things from various materials, weaving, designing graphic patterns, and playing with color. Because of a strong interest in science I considered going into medical illustration, but the lure of textiles led me to the Syracuse University College of Visual and Performing Arts program in textiles/surface pattern design, where I received a BFA in 1976. I freelanced in the industry for a while but then pursued my interest in science and returned for a degree in astrophysics. Currently I build instrumentation for radio astronomy.

I still enjoy working in many areas of textile arts (quilting, weaving, bobbin lace, knitting, and clothing construction, just to name a few), and what I learn from one, I apply to the others. I tend to be process oriented and enjoy working on something with my hands and figuring out how to do it. I often explore new techniques in quilting, some garnered from magazines or books, and some I develop myself. I have been quilting for approximately 12 years.

The Collaboration

This is our second collaboration. People ask us, "Collaboration? How does that work? Who gets the quilt?"

Collaboration is like any dialogue, with shared ideas, responses, revisions, and questions. The fabric was Ann's (she has more stripes than she realized). The designing all had to be done at her house because once the fabric was put on her design wall, there was no easy way to move it. We live about a 15-minute drive apart.

Leaf Cycle 65" x 65"

It's terrifically exciting for an artist to have a like mind to work with, like playing a duet instead of a solo.

The idea of having two sizes of blocks was Ronna's. After our first get-together for a "cutting party," as Ronna called it, things seemed exciting but the direction we were going in was totally unknown. There was no real plan. After the first day, it looked like this.

Ann made an initial, experimental drawing, attempting to pull something together out of the many possibilities that suggested themselves. At that stage, we thought it would be more interesting to have the curves and diagonals offset, discontinuous.

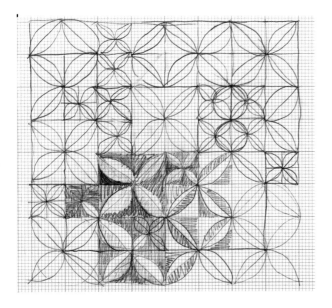

Eventually some shapes emerged on the design wall that we liked, formed by either hue or value. We revised our drawing when we realized there was better flow and balance if the pattern was not offset. The diagonals and curves were much more beautiful when continuous.

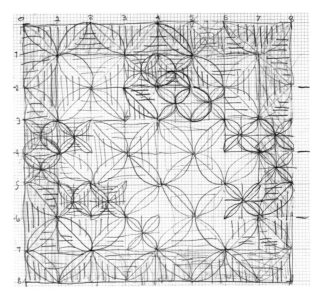

The idea of a center yellow circle was Ann's; it formed a seasonal progression from the center outwards. Certain areas just seemed to become the province of one or the other of us: the little blue circles just above the center are Ronna's; the little red circles at the right are Ann's. The idea of a dark border was Ann's, and she was the one who overdyed some fabrics dark green because we just didn't have enough fabric that was green enough or dark enough.

Some areas remained settled and certain from the beginning, while other areas were in flux until the very end. If one of us didn't like something—some choice of color, or group of colors—we would indicate that there seemed to be a problem, and the solution to the problem could come from either of us. Many extra leaf halves were generated in attempting to balance the color, yet keep it exciting and flowing from one area to another.

Ann's striped fabric is roughly seasonally organized into winter piles of blues and purples, summery greens, fall oranges and ochers. Ann had thought of the quilt as summery, primarily green, since it was started in the summer. Ronna dived into some of the other piles and used colors—teals and purples—that Ann would not have considered using. Ann was taken aback at first, then pleased with the effect, and she too started including fabrics that seemed far from the major notes of the quilt. Those openings of one's assumptions or prejudices are one of the great things about collaborating.

There were times when we had disagreements about certain areas, and it was challenging to come up with solutions that pleased both of us. There were times when one of us didn't like something and the other had to persuade her that it really did work in the quilt. There were times when we were both very excited about our progress, which does seem to go much, much faster than when working alone.

The quilt is definitely not what either of us might have initially envisioned, or what we would have made if we were working alone. But we both like it very much! It's terrifically exciting for an artist to have a like mind to work with, like playing a duet instead of a solo.

As to who gets the quilt, well, we're both more process oriented than product oriented (though we like setting goals and reaching them). And the accumulation of striped fabric over the years, well, that *was* all Ann's.

Technique

The basis of our technique for this quilt is pretty standard freezer-paper appliqué. Freezer paper is ironed to the wrong side of the leaf. A basting stitch is run along the area of the leaf that will be turned under.

The basting thread is pulled to gather the seam allowance against the paper.

Then the seam allowance is pressed.

We fold under the excess fabric at the point and machine baste downward from the point to hold the fabric in place.

Fingers, not pins, are all that's needed to hold the corners in place as a few long basting stitches are taken. There is none of the distortion that you'd get if you used pins to hold the fabric down, and the resulting points are more precise. The long, loose basting stitches are easy to undo after appliquéing. We appliquéd using a blanket stitch and polyester monofilament. We cut out the backs of the blocks to release the freezer paper.

Photo by A. Guerrero

Finalist
Peggy Fetterhoff
The Woodlands, Texas

Meet Peggy

I was born in Pennsylvania but grew up in Niagara Falls, New York. I moved to Houston, Texas, in 1974 where I raised my four children. I put myself through college while they were growing up, earning a BBA in finance from the University of Houston. I've been sewing since I was 12 years old, mainly focused on clothing and home decor items. After the children left home, the empty nest syndrome resulted in my finding new and interesting ways to enrich my life. The discovery of quilting was part of that enrichment.

In 1995, I met my neighbor Jan Thompson in a quilt store and she introduced me to the world of quilting. Jan also provided my first lesson on hand quilting. I found it relaxing and cheaper than a psychiatrist in dealing with a very stressful job.

One day while shopping for fabric, I found a book on watercolor quilts that became my inspiration. My first watercolor contest quilt was FLORAL PHANTASMA. It had over 4,000 two-inch squares, more than 1,000 different fabrics, and was hand quilted. It was juried into the AQS Quilt Show and Contest in Paducah in 1998, later won several prizes in other contests, and was included in the PBS video *America Quilts.*

After moving into my current home, I talked my youngest son and my brother into converting half of my second floor into a custom studio for my quilting. It was the first time in my life I had my own room for sewing. My quilt studio alone is an inspiration, with a custom sewing cabinet, custom tables that can be moved and joined to the cabinet, 58 drawers in one room, and three different size design walls.

I retired in July of 2009 from an information technology network engineering position. I take a long time to make my quilts—18 months to five years for the quilts I have entered in past contests. It is only now with more time that I can make a quilt within a year's time. I started my NQOF entry in February and finished in October—really fast for me. That is always everyone's favorite question to ask at competition: "How long did it take for you to make it?"

Inspiration

The inspiration for my art is a reflection of the way I view the world. I visualize color everywhere in curving perspectives. Fabric is my paint! I have always loved art but did not realize I had any artistic talent until I discovered colorwash or watercolor quilts.

Deirdre Amsden's Colorwash technique and Pat Maixner Magaret and Donna Ingram Slusser's book *Watercolor Quilts* (see Resources, page 93) have been influential in the way I create fiber art. My pieces have many of the elements and characteristics of Impressionist paintings. By combining large numbers of different fabrics with varied patterns and colors, I am able to create unusual and original designs. The fabric pieces can take on any size and shape, from squares to hexagons, that allow the designs to flow in multiple directions. The final fiber art creation is a unique design originating from this creative process.

The Orange Peel block was interesting to me because of the possibilities and challenges that curves provide. I researched the various patterns classified as Orange Peel and found the basic concept of using a circle sectioned

Oh, The Web We Weave 59" x 58"

*The inspiration for my art is a reflection
of the way I view the world. I visualize color
everywhere in curving perspectives.*

with four inner quarter circle curves within a block. I created a basic drawing of multiple circles within a square and focused on how the circles of the same size overlap. I also found with this first step that the squares are eliminated when you start overlapping circles of different sizes.

I decided to use rusty orange fabrics combined with browns—not colors I usually work with—which required a lot of new fabric purchases. This was a great excuse, even though I didn't need one, to add to my fabric collection. For every project I am working on I carry a muslin strip with small pieces of fabric sewn on that enables me to find correct shades and color hues. I combine the new fabric with the large collection I already have so that I end up with hundreds of quarter yard or one-third yard pieces of fabric to choose from for each project.

I usually create a few drawings on graph paper, but the design never truly comes together until I start putting fabric on my design wall. The inspiration for all my designs is driven by the fabric itself. I prefer commercial fabric to making my own because there is such a large variety to choose from to stimulate my imagination.

The initial drawing for this design included four small circles of the same size within a square block. The joining of the four circles created a fifth circle in the center, which ended up in the final design in the center of each web when the four webs were joined together.

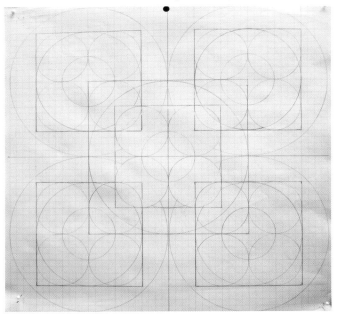

The biggest challenge of the design was overlaying each row of circles so that there were no gaps in the background. The problem was not apparent as the curve of the circle expanded but only as the curve of the circle decreased. If you look closely, you will see that there are three quarter parts of each orange circle overlapping the previous row, eliminating the need for the fourth quarter of the circle. This required some adjustments in the placement of each row of circles. It also required sometimes changing the quarter circles to a smaller size to leave enough of the background centers visible.

Layouts were created on paper, made into fabric, then disposed of when they did not work. After discovering an arrangement that did work, I made template plastic layouts to ensure that the fabric circles were the same for each of the four sections.

Technique

I started this project at a quilt retreat in Texas. It is hard for me to start a project in front of my quilt friends because I have a very strict rule, especially in the early stages, that no one can comment, good or bad. Even the smallest remark can change what I am doing and not always for the good. The rare exception to this is when I am completely stuck on some aspect of the project and have no idea how to fix the element that is causing problems. Then I seek suggestions from quilter friends or my daughter, Debra, whose judgment I trust because they also sew.

I use acrylic quilt templates both for drawing and for cutting out fabric with different size rotary cutters, depending on how thick the templates are. I purchased additional circle templates so that I have sizes ranging from 1" to 16" in ½" increments.

The use of many shades of orange fabrics in the quarter circles creates the color changes from the smaller 1" inner circles, which are the lightest, to the larger outer 8" circles, which are the darkest. The brown fabric centers of the circles are also arranged from light to dark to accentuate the shading.

I decided to use fused interfacing both because of time and the spacing between the quarter circles and the circle background. I had never fused interfacing on quilt fabric before, as I am a hand quilter. This required experimenting with every type of fusible I could find for a workable solution to create this design. The requirements included being able to draw the quarter circles on the fusible interfacing, being able to reposition each circle with a sticky backing, and being light enough for several layers to overlap.

Templates were created for each row of circles to assist with an accurate layout. The largest row for the outside of each section was not fused until it was added to the background. As each set of circles was machine raw-edge appliquéd, they looked like spider webs, which is what influenced the name of the quilt, Oh, The Web We Weave.

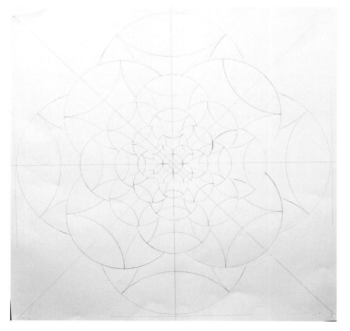

The next challenge was how to combine the four webs. A pattern emerged by joining the four webs together that showed the original circle block design in five places. The center had a quarter from each of the four webs; then two quarters were added to each of the four outside integrating circles that extend into the borders.

In choosing colors for the borders, it was apparent that the same color intensity had to be used so the colors complemented the many rusty orange fabrics but were not overwhelmed by them. The yellow/gold in the fabric borders is every bit as bold as the orange. The black background fabric has gold/brown threads running through it to further integrate with the orange and brown in the cen-

ter. Additional fabric colors in green, yellow, and black were added to the centers of the five integrating circles so the same colors could be repeated in the multiple borders. The four joined webs were overlaid on the multiple inner borders with fusing and machine appliqué.

The 4"–12" acrylic circle templates were used again to create the outer orange flares in each corner. By adding a yellow fabric piece in the center of each set of corner flares, it appears as though the yellow border is extended into the center of the flares. The same yellow/gold and print fabric is repeated in the outer borders.

Because of the fusing, the hand quilting is outlined in and around the quarter circles in the webs. More extensive hand-quilting designs are added to the corners and borders. The quilting thread color is a rusty medium shade of brown to accentuate the various colors of fabric in the art piece.

Photo by Mick Forey

Finalist
Linda Forey
Montreal, Quebec, Canada

Meet Linda

I've sewn all my life, helped by having a father who was a custom, bespoke, shirt tailor, and who had a very fast industrial sewing machine at home. I started with doll clothes, then graduated through soft toys to clothes for myself. Though I made my first small wallhanging in 1986 while living temporarily in Connecticut, I didn't start properly quilting until the early '90s when I moved to Toulouse, France.

There I met a group of ladies from the United States and Europe who made a raffle quilt every year for the Christmas Fair. Failing to win it by buying raffle tickets, I decided I would have to make my own! Returning to England in 1996, I enrolled in the City and Guilds course in patchwork and quilting. I happily spent the next five years immersed in parts one and two of the course. It involved a single day at college each week, but my husband swears it was full-time.

In 2003 I became a founding member of a small group of quilters in the United Kingdom called TextileARTS, formed with the idea of exhibiting our quilts in art galleries. We successfully had exhibitions in 2004, 2006, and 2007, and I learned a lot from the experience. In 2008, my husband moved to Montreal, and later that year I joined him. Suddenly freed of children, gardening, and housework, I've been able to devote more of my time to quilting.

I have always been drawn to radially symmetrical quilts, and love the mathematics involved in complex designs. I also love working with different, more unconventional, fabrics. But though I often buy brightly colored fabrics, I find many of my more successful quilts feature more subdued hues. Gray and black fabrics appear regularly in my work.

Inspiration and Design

I've tried designing quilts for the NQOF competition before, but never completed one to my satisfaction. This year the design somersaulted into my head almost full grown as soon as I looked at the Orange Peel block. Often used in ancient tile patterns, the design of squares forming a circle can be traced back to medieval times. Often used with 12 squares, signifying the 12 signs of the zodiac, when the ratio of one square to the next is root 2, any number of squares, from 5 upwards, can be used to form this type of pattern. The mathematics gets more complex with repeats other than 12, so I wrote a simple spreadsheet to calculate the size and position of each square, starting with a 1" square for the first round.

Thus for 5 squares, each is inclined at an angle of 72 degrees, and the size of squares and the diameters of the circles on which they sit, in inches, are:

Size of square	1.00	4.52	20.43	92.35
Diameter	2.41	10.88	49.16	222.21

As you can see, the size of the square increases extremely fast, as does the diameter of the circles on which they sit, meaning there are large blank areas between each square.

For 12 squares each is inclined at 30 degrees, and the corresponding sizes are:

1.00	1.41	2.00	2.83	4.00	5.66
5.46	7.73	10.93	15.45	21.86	30.91

Now the sizes increase relatively slowly, but the diameter of the first circle is comparatively large.

Full Circle 57" x 57"

I have always been drawn to radially symmetrical quilts, and love the mathematics involved in complex designs.

With CorelDRAW® software, I drew examples of the pattern using a variety of numbers of squares, coloring some in to see how the pattern worked when the Orange Peel block was used.

I felt 12 was too complex and confusing for the viewer and though I liked the odd number examples, the coloring possibilities of these lacked any symmetry and balance. I finally settled on 10 squares in the circle; this seemed to give me the balance I wanted, without the too rigid appearance that arose with just 8 squares.

The final step for the design was to choose appropriate colors. I wanted to use some of the many silks I have bought in my travels around the world, especially the ones with "shot" colors (different colors used for the warp and weft when woven), but couldn't decide on the colors for the squares and their background. The design sat on my desk for weeks as I failed to get the inspiration I wanted, until I walked into a fabric shop one day and saw a black fabric with a tiny silver dot/ sparkle. Suddenly it all made sense—the squares needed to be black to show up the silks to their best advantage, and the background needed to be neutral so as not to distract the viewer from the Orange Peel block itself.

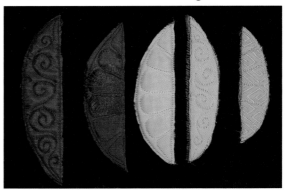

The quilting design was more problematic. One of the problems was the change in scale between the squares. It was hard to find a pattern that I could put into a 1" square, and yet still be interesting in a 14" square. Eventually I went back to the basic Orange Peel block, tried rotating it by about 30 degrees, and put it back into the pieced Orange Peel square. Now I could change the scale by simply putting more repeats of the same pattern, and the quilting echoed the design of the whole quilt by spiraling in toward a center.

Techniques

My first inclination for the Orange Peel square was to make it using bias-rolled edges as in the Cathedral Windows technique. I made a couple of samples, and though the technique worked well for the smaller squares, by the time the squares were over 14", the rolled edges just disappeared and were indistinguishable from an appliquéd section.

On top of this, I had to make the edges of the square from a double layer of fabric folded on the bias, which meant I needed well over four times the fabric, for no appreciable reward. I abandoned the notion and used simple appliqué to add the silk sections.

Although the silks were slippery, I did not want to fuse stabilizer to them. So I elected to use freezer-paper templates. Each template was ironed onto the wrong side of the silk, then the edge needle-turned and hand appliquéd to the black square. As the silk frayed badly, I used larger than normal seam allowances and, as some of the silks were so thin, left the black square intact behind the silk.

Each completed square was joined to a corresponding background section using set-in seams. I found a few hand stitches at the corner helped to get a perfect match. I could then join the units together relatively easily.

I had decided to use machine trapunto to emphasize the pattern and to make up for my disappointment that the rolled-edges concept had failed. I layered the complete quilt onto a wool batting. Initially I drew the entire quilting design in chalk before layering the quilt, but found all the chalk had disappeared before I started the quilting. So I drew the quilting pattern on each block just before it was quilted with threads that continued the colors of the silk. I had planned to use very little quilting on the silk pieces, but the larger pieces of the thin fabric slumped. I added extra quilting in a transparent thread, which solved the problem, even though it slightly altered the look of the shot silk itself.

Cutting away the extra batting took two long days.

Finally the quilt was layered onto a cotton batting, backed, and the background areas quilted very simply to flatten them.

Photo by quilt show passer-by

Finalist
Julia Graber
Brooksville, Mississippi

Meet Julia

I have been a quiltmaker since my early 20s and started making innovative quilts in my 40s. I grew up in Virginia on the banks of North River with six sisters and one brother. We enjoyed the great out-of-doors, climbing the bluff, making houses in the woods, canoeing, and swimming. In the winter we enjoyed sledding and skating. We also learned to work, milking the cow by hand, mowing the lawn, working in the garden and harvesting its fruits.

After graduating from high school I worked at a local printing business doing typesetting and layout. Then I went to Red Lake, Ontario, Canada, and helped in a children's home as needed. We took weekly turns doing the laundry, cooking, taking care of the babies, doing activities with the older children, and night duty.

In 1973 I came to Mississippi and taught grades 6–8 at our Magnolia Christian Day School for three years. It was here that I met and then married Paul Graber. We have six children and now four grandchildren who live close by. We live on a farm and raise corn, soybeans, and a little wheat, and feed out 3,200 head of hogs at a time for Prestage Farms. Paul also helps his brother operate our trucking company where I help in the office. We are members of Magnolia Mennonite Church and enjoy the fellowship and activities of our local brotherhood, as well as mission activities in Romania.

Each year my Heatwole family and relatives enjoy getting together for a week of quilting, sewing, food, fun, and fellowship. We laugh a lot together and stay up late and just plain down have a good time. I like to see all the projects that eventually get displayed on the walls to show for the week's activities.

I also enjoy traveling to lecture on my quiltmaking and I love to teach workshops in our home. It's a fun day to have the living room full of humming sewing machines and chatting quilters who love doing what I am doing. We'll then have lunch together, with the afternoon to keep on sewing.

Visit my blog http://pauljuliagraber.xanga.com/ to learn more about my life and how I just don't have enough time to sew and quilt!

Recently my sisters Polly and Barbara and I have been giving Microsoft® PowerPoint® presentations on "Our Quilting Journeys" and sharing our quilts with others at guild meetings and shows. We three started a blog to share with others our joys of piecing and making quilts. Visit us at http://threemennonitequiltingsisters.blogspot.com/

Inspiration and Design

I so much enjoy the challenge of taking an old familiar quilt block and turning it into something new and innovative. For this year's Orange Peel block, I Googled for images of the block and also searched Barbara Brackman's *Encyclopedia of Pieced Quilt Patterns* (see Resources, page 93). I played with the images in Electric Quilt software with different blocks and layouts and colors, but nothing really appealed to me there. I finally decided to try a polar grid (circular graph), and made a few hand drawings of what I had in my head, and that seemed to work.

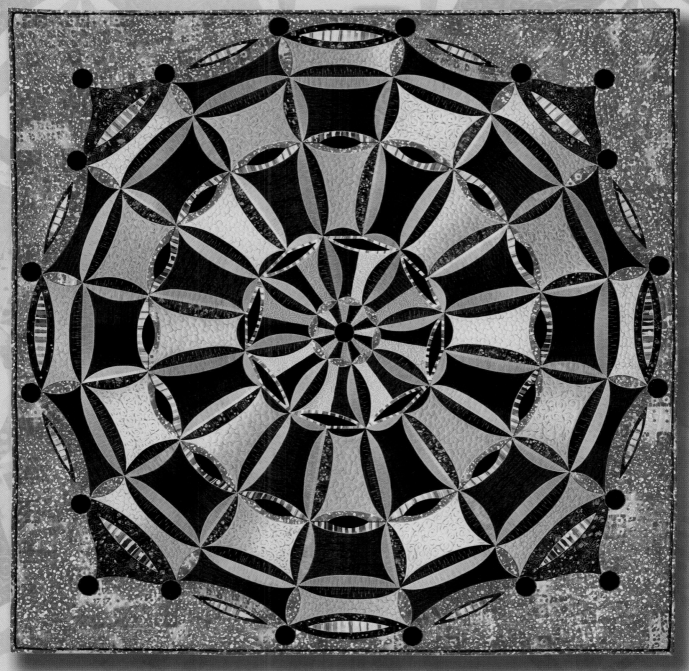

I'm really drawn to bright and bold colors along with strong geometric shapes and lines.

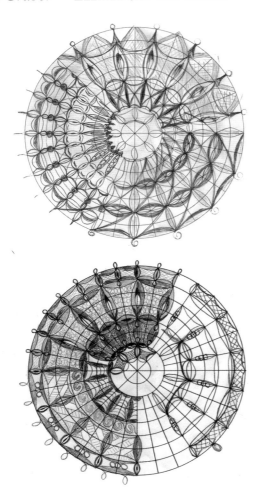

I'm really drawn to bright and bold colors along with strong geometric shapes and lines, and I like a high contrast in value. The shades of orange, yellow, purple, and black in tone-on-tone and batik fabrics are all appealing to me.

My quilt represents the wheels within a wheel described in Ezekiel 10:9 & 10. "And as for their appearances, they four had one likeness, as if a wheel had been in the midst of a wheel." The Old Testament book of Ezekiel describes the prophet Ezekiel's visions and warnings of judgment and the fall of Jerusalem and the temple, as well as his prophesies of salvation and the Lord returning to a new temple. Chapter 10 specifically describes his visions of God's glory departing from the temple and the "whirling wheels" and cherubim that accompanied Him as He left. The colors of the quilt represent the fire that was within

the wheels (verse 6) and the regal glory of God. The circles represent the outer eyes on the wheels described in verse 12, "...the wheels, were full of eyes round about...."

Techniques

Piecing

To form the base of my Orange Peel quilt, I cut long strips in a variety of widths of the orange/yellow and purple fabrics and sewed them together.

From these strip-sets I cut 16 wedges and placed them on my "design floor" to form a circle and sewed them together. My grandson, Ashton, found the wheel fascinating and loved playing on it.

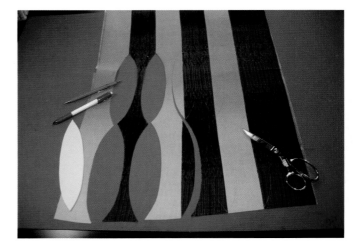

Next I sewed more alternating colors of strips together and fused the strip-set to a stabilizer. Using the Orange Peel design, I cut a template from a manila folder, placed it on the fused fabric strip-set, drew around it, and cut out the "peels."

I fused the cutouts to my base.

I cut out more and more Orange Peel motifs from additional fabric and fused them to the base. Next I added black fabric for variety.

I continued in this fashion, fused the wheel onto the background, and added more Orange Peel motifs and circles.

After the quilt was finished I asked family and friends to help choose a name. Ezekiel Saw the Wheel seemed very fitting; so then I decided to add "Ezekiel" in the bottom right corner.

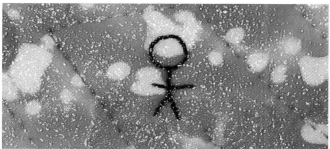

Blocking

One big frustration for me was the way the quilt wanted to buckle from all the heavy machine appliqué and fusing. To help make it lie flat, I blocked it on my living room floor on top of a piece of upholstery vinyl. I poured a gallon of water over the quilt and patted it down good to make sure all the fibers from the top, batting, and backing were sopping wet. I put the fan to it and left it to air dry for a day or two. Later I blocked it again adding Elmer's® School Glue to the water to help stiffen it up.

I felt quite honored and happy when my quilt won three blue ribbons at the Pine Belt Quilters, Inc., 13th Biennial Fiber Art & Quilt Show in Hattiesburg, Mississippi.

Photo by Kimberly Iafolla

Finalist
Amy Krasnansky
Baltimore, Maryland

Meet Amy

I wanted to be an artist when I grew up. I drew pictures and painted and tried calligraphy. I was the child who actually finished those embroidery kits of flowers and puppies and kittens, the child who stank up the house with oil paints. I was also the child who spilled black ink on her bedroom carpet. Twice.

My mother taught me to sew, first by hand and then with her machine. (Perhaps she was trying to distract me from making things with paint and ink.) From pillows and doll clothes, I graduated to clothes for real people. My long-suffering mother at least pretended that she liked the lumpy skirt I made for her when I was eleven.

An artist: that was clearly an impractical goal. Besides, by high school I could see that plenty of kids were better at art than I was. And I had Computer Nerd written all over me, so I studied electrical engineering in college (not a bad choice) and worked for several years writing software. After my children were born, I stopped working full time, leaving more time for childcare, projects, and not doing housework. I like gardening and do-it-yourself home improvement. I have also deluded myself into believing that I will write a publishable young adult fantasy novel at some point in my life. So projects are not hard to find.

I started quilting about 10 years ago when my nephew was born. I wanted to make him a quilt in yellows and greens. A few Log Cabin blocks later, I was hooked. I enjoyed the sense of progress that came from chain piecing the blocks—so much easier than making clothing. I loved using lots of different fabrics and combining blocks to create unexpected designs. Over the next few months, I checked out every quilting book in the Baltimore County library system. Did I mention I'm a nerd?

I love to challenge myself, and so far quilting has offered those challenges—always another idea or technique that I want to try. A couple of years ago, I began showing quilts in the Maryland State Fair. A few ribbons and the support of the women in my Bible study group gave me the confidence to enter the New Quilts from an Old Favorite contest. I'm glad I did.

More Fun Facts:

I have sworn never again to lay tile (fun to design, but hard on the knees); braid a rug (boring); upholster anything more complicated than a dining room chair (I can't remember why not); or do a counted cross-stitch (such a pretty picture, but it took two years to finish).

Projects that I will probably never finish include a trapunto dragon on shiny taffeta that shows pin marks and doesn't show my markings; a needlepoint of hummingbirds that started warping partway through; a landscape that failed at the quilting stage; and a freezer-paper appliqué of fish turning into birds à la Escher that just got too tedious.

I live in Baltimore with my husband, two children, a cat, and a lurking horde of dust bunnies.

Under A Peel:
Don't Judge a Quilt by Its Cover 75" x 75"

I love to challenge myself, and so far quilting
has offered those challenges—always another
idea or technique that I want to try.

Inspiration and Design

What do quilts, oranges, and Shrek have in common? They all have layers. Quilts by definition are layered in both form (backing, batting, top) and design (piecing/appliqué pattern, fabric choice, borders, quilting).

Under a Peel: Don't Judge a Quilt By Its Cover is a quilt about quilts. Its batting is exposed, revealing the layered form of the quilt. One of the repeating blocks is an Orange Peel superimposed on itself, suggesting the layering of design. The geometric abstraction rests on top of a realistic orange (admittedly oversized), implying the source of its inspiration.

I designed the geometric portion of the quilt using Electric Quilt software, playing with the Orange Peel block, modifying it, and combining it with other blocks. Finally, I created the block that superimposed one Orange Peel on top of another. I layered the small-

er block on top of the larger block by darkening the colors where the blocks overlapped. Then I alternated this superimposed block with a block containing four smaller Orange Peels. The combination formed circles that reminded me of oranges.

I liked my nine circles, but I wanted to link the geometric design to its real-world inspiration—oranges and the peeling thereof. The large orange in the border serves as a foundation for the abstract portion of the quilt. The batting exposed for the interior of the fruit emphasizes the connection between the layers of an orange and the layers of a quilt.

Freeform quilting in the border strengthens the representation of the orange and contrasts with the geometric design in the rest of the quilt. Orange branches fill the background area. In the geometric portion of the quilt, I chose a repeating pattern that echoes the leaves on the orange branches and the shape of the Orange Peel block.

Fun Facts (that expose me as a rank amateur):
- To transfer the border piecing pattern from my computer to fabric, I printed out 18 pages, trimmed, and glued them together. That was only half. I flipped it over to do the other half of the border.

- The orange batting does not go all the way through the quilt. It is whipstitched to natural-colored batting just past the seam allowances. All my light-colored patches looked orange when placed on top of orange batting, so I had to improvise. Yes, the quilt is a phony. It pretends to be open and honest about its batting, but it's really showing you a colored view of its inner self.

- While marking the top for quilting, I accidentally grabbed a permanent pen instead of the air-soluble marking pen. I drew a few strokes before realizing what I had done. After mentally cursing myself, I decided that maybe the lines wouldn't show after I quilted over them. They showed. I unpicked all the stitches that held that patch to the quilt and sewed in a replacement patch. Bless that clear monofilament thread. I bet you can't find the spot. And that wasn't even the worst "uh-oh" moment...

I was using warm water to wash off some water-soluble stabilizer I had used to mark the quilting. The water started turning orange. I had forgotten that the hand-dyed batting and backing should only be washed in cold water. Ack! I switched to cold water, but it was too late. A couple of light-colored patches had absorbed the dye. Good thing I knew how to replace a patch.

• I had to photograph the quilt while squatting on our waterbed (it faced the only large wall with good lighting) and ship my entry overnight because I did not finish until just before the entry deadline.

Technique

Trust a software engineer to do quilting the techie way. Instead of drawing an orange cut in half and tilted sideways, or photographing and tracing a real orange, I modeled it in a 3-D drawing program.

I used a free program called Blender (See Resources page 93). You can download it to your computer from www.blender.org. There are many online tutorials, and you will need them if you want to use it.

I started with a sphere, which is shown here viewed from the top.

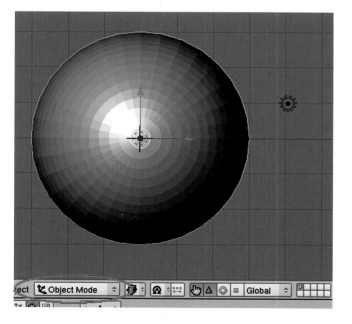

Through a series of steps I created a tilted decapitated sphere.

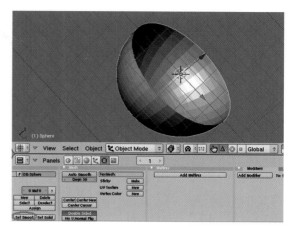

It was a little bumpy, but the Set Smooth button took care of that.

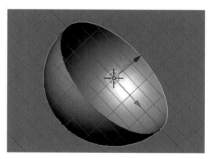

Isn't that lovely?

I traced the model into my quilting program and completed my design.

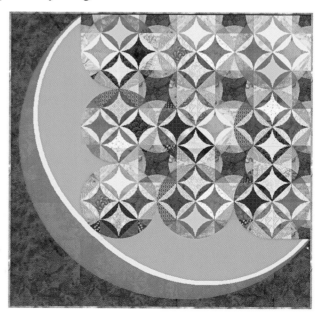

Finalists

Ree Moffitt
Palmer, Alaska

Photo by Mark R. Simpson Photography

Sheilah Crum
Palmer, Alaska

Meet Ree

I'm a lifetime resident of Alaska, born here eight years before statehood, the oldest of four children. We were raised on a 40-acre homestead at the base of Pioneer Peak in the Knik River valley. No one in my family was a quilter but my mother was a very talented seamstress and taught me how to sew as a young child. I in turn taught her how to quilt when she was in her sixties.

My first quilting experiences were wholecloth baby quilts but nothing resembled a pieced quilt other than one I started 40 years ago out of leftover double knits that remains unfinished to this day. My first UFO of many!

In 1980 my mother-in-law brought me a bag of quilt magazines and I was hooked. My early years of clothing construction, cake decorating, drafting classes, and 13 years of operating an upholstery business all helped me develop skills that were later helpful in quilting. Until recent years, with working and raising a family, my quilts were few and far between and all were tied or hand quilted.

In 1999 I closed my upholstery shop and promptly converted it into a quilting studio. I joined the local Valley Quilters Guild, and five years later found myself working again at Sylvia's Quilt Depot in Wasilla. I love the camaraderie of being around other quilters. We all seem to draw inspiration from one another.

My interests in quiltmaking are constantly changing but not slowing down. I enjoy the design process as much if not more than the actual quiltmaking and have to admit to being more of a piecer than a quilter. Lately curved piecing using freezer-paper templates has held my interest and I have more designs in my head and on paper than I'll ever have time to make.

Meet Sheilah

For as long as I can remember I've had a fascination with fabrics. I remember playing with the pedal on my grandmother's treadle sewing machine when I was very young. One of my most prized possessions is a Double Wedding Ring quilt made of feed sacks from the early 1930s that was made by my great-grandmother. Maybe I have some cotton in my DNA because both of my grandmothers were quilters.

My mother taught me how to use her sewing machine, and, by the time I was 8 years old, I was making clothing for my dolls and quickly transitioned to making very simple A-line shifts for myself. I was very surprised as a young girl to hear that some of my friends didn't know how to sew or even have a sewing machine, because I thought a sewing machine was just like an oven or a refrigerator—everyone had one.

I made my first quilt back in the '70s using green and the much-maligned color orange. To this very day, orange has a special place in my quilting heart and is a valued color in most of my quilts. Fabrics were not of the same quality as they are today and when I washed my quilt, the green dye bled all over the orange. I was so devastated that I didn't make another quilt for about 18 years. This also set the stage for my practice of washing every fabric in my stash.

My mother-in-law came to visit us in 1995 and brought some quilt blocks she was making. I thought it would be fun to sew with her. I bought fabrics for my second quilt, of course, orange again, and I have not stopped collecting quilt fabrics since.

In 1997, I purchased a very much-used fourth-hand short-arm quilt machine as a way to help save money for my

Color Splash 64" x 64"

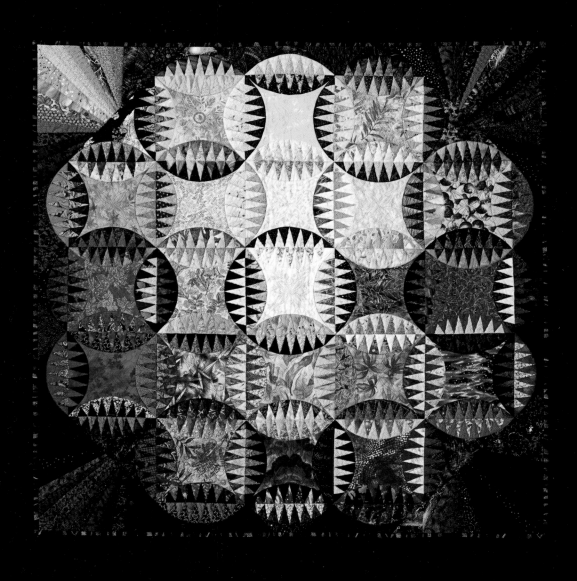

Indian Orange Peel pattern by Karen K. Stone

The biggest challenge in making this quilt was choosing and working with so many warm-colored fabrics.

quilting habit and quickly started quilting for friends and for charity. At the time, we were building a house and my husband very graciously gave up the third bay of the three-car garage for my machine. The more I quilted the more I became fascinated by the ability to "draw" with thread. The free-moving quilting machine gave me the ability to work outside the confines of the seam allowance and feed dogs. Quilts became a canvas for me to draw on.

I replaced my shortarm with a full-size longarm after visiting Houston Quilt Festival in 2003 and test-driving every machine then on the market. About three years ago I purchased a computerized system for my longarm, and, in many ways, it has opened a new world to me. I now run my own machine-quilting business and teach quilting at a local quilt store. I love working with clients in developing design ideas for finishing their quilts. I, in turn, am inspired by their quilts. I have put my quilt signature on about 1,500 quilts. It is a truly awesome thought for me that 50 years or so from now, long after I'm gone, the granddaughter of a client will probably use a quilt that I had some hand in.

Inspiration and Design–Ree

When I first heard of the Orange Peel contest theme earlier this year, I already had the center section of this quilt top completed. So instead of setting out to make my quilt for this contest, it was as if the contest came along just in time for my quilt top.

From the day I came across Joen Wolfrom's book *Color Play: Easy Steps to Imaginative Color in Quilts*, I was inspired to make a color wheel quilt. The inspiration for COLOR SPLASH pretty much came from the color wheel itself, Joen's book, and Karen K. Stone's Indian Orange Peel pattern (see Resources, page 93).

My first color wheel quilt was a Tessellated Star design, but the quilt generally lacked the depth, texture, and value changes that I was looking for. I needed a medallion-style layout that could be divided equally by 12. One morning I woke up with a dream still in my head— my color wheel quilt had come to life!

The biggest challenge in making this quilt was choosing and working with so many warm-colored fabrics. Now that it is finished, I find it ironic that the same warm-hued section I had so much trouble selecting fabrics for is my favorite part of the quilt!

Technique—Ree

I used many techniques from start to finish. What first began as a simple idea to make a color wheel quilt went through many phases over the years it took to complete. Once I had decided on the Orange Peel block, I sketched my outline drawing to graph paper. Using colored pencils I began drawing circles with black and gray where I wanted them to dominate and filled in the colors with the tints toward the center. After many variations, I liked what I saw. The corner fan blades came next.

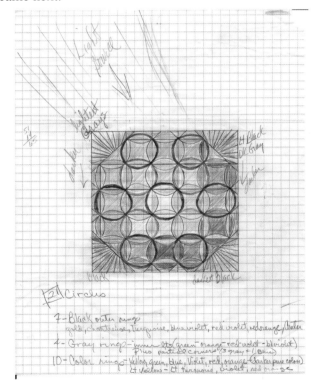

I found an Orange Peel block in EQ that worked. I set the size to 9", divided the base of the arc into nine 1" segments, and drew in evenly spaced spikes. I printed the pattern pieces on lightweight newsprint *without* seam allowances; it is easier to pin the intersecting points when sewing the blocks together and there is less paper to remove after the seams are sewn.

I traced my printouts of the four 12" corner blocks to the paper side of freezer paper after lining up and taping the pattern pages together. I pressed the fabric to the waxy side of the freezer paper to secure it and continued to fold back the freezer paper at each stitching line when I added another ray of fabric to the fans.

I met Sheilah at the shop one day to get her advice on the border and it didn't take her long to find the perfect muted gold-on-black striped fabric for a narrow separator border that I used for the binding as well. It was time to get busy on it so I could get the top to Sheilah in time to quilt when she got home from the Valdez Quilt Festival. She only had a month to work her magic and get it back to me to bind, have photographed, and get the entry form in on time for the contest.

Quilting Design—Sheilah

I have my mind in two worlds—the traditional and the artistic. I like freeform geometric and artistic designs, but I also love feathered wreaths and borders. The perfection of a very detailed digitized design is amazing. I know that I am offering my clients the best that I can do with the most innovative technology available. I enjoy using a combination of freehand and digitized patterns. More recently I have taken my own designs and digitized them using a computer-aided drafting program.

I selected digital Heirloom Lace designs from designer Donna Kleinke of One Song Needle Arts (see Resources, page 93). The Sawtooth points of the melon piecing were done freehand using my wavy line outline. I like using this method to substitute for stitch in the ditch because it serves the purpose of an outline without the tedium of using a ruler and gives the quilt a bit of movement at the same time. I used this method on the corners radiating out from the center. I felt putting a design motif in those areas would compete with Ree's design.

I prefer to use design and color choices, which is why I used 22 different threads on Ree's quilt, so they would blend rather than compete. I chose and quilted a very elaborate ornamental border design, but in black. This served the purpose of drawing viewers into the quilt,

making them come in for a closer look to see what they got a hint of farther away. It was very much an honor to work on Ree's quilt, and further an honor for her quilt to be selected as a finalist.

Finalists

 *Claudia Clark Myers*

Duluth, Minnesota

Photo by Thomas T. Myers, III

 *Marilyn Badger*

Saint George, Utah

Photo by Hartley B. Badger

Meet Claudia

Many quilters and friends know that I began quilting after retiring from opera, ballet, and theater costume designing; that I had a Victorian pillow business, Confections; and that I started my working life as a floral designer. But they may not know that in addition to being a dedicated quilter, I am also an antique dealer.

This is a part of my life that, in addition to teaching me to sew, was a special gift from my mother—a love of antiques, the curiosity to find out about them, and the enjoyment of the hunt. I remember many late nights, seeing her at the kitchen table surrounded by her reference books, trying to identify a particular piece, cold cup of coffee beside her, loupe attached to her glasses, writing for all she was worth. I still have, and use, her loupe.

Her area of expertise was glass and china but mine is antique and vintage jewelry. I believe that jewelry is usually connected to the happiest times in our lives. Some of the jewelry designs have inspired my quiltmaking, and sometimes I even sew it on my quilts for embellishment, like the copper bracelet links on JUICY FRUIT. Thanks, Mom.

Meet Marilyn

While living on our boat in Southern California in the late 1970s, I started receiving *Quilters Newsletter* magazine and I was hooked. There is so much more variety in the quilting world today compared with when I started. When you attend the major quilt shows around the country every year and see all the beautiful quilts in the competitions, it's impossible not to be inspired.

Quilting has pretty much taken over my life. My husband will vouch for that! I try to fit other things into my quilting schedule—golf, working out, and all the other necessities in life such as cooking, cleaning, shopping, and just enjoying being outside in the sunshine every chance I get.

Although I'm known as a machine quilter, I love to piece. I began by piecing my own quilts and hiring others to quilt them. Piecing is and always has been my therapy. When I'm quilting on a competition piece, I get into what I call "The Zone." I am thinking about and working on that quilt 24/7 until it is completed. After two to three months of that (which is the amount of time it takes me to complete a quilt), sitting down and piecing or appliquéing a quilt top is very relaxing.

Inspiration and Design: Claudia

My quilt projects almost always start with the fabrics and colors. The New Quilts from an Old Favorite challenge is different because you are given a starting point with the traditional block that is chosen. The most familiar version of the Orange Peel block is pretty straightforward. Other versions looked more interesting, and when I found one I hadn't seen before, in Maggie Malone's book *5,500 Quilt Block Designs* (#3872, page 299), I decided to start with that.

Juicy Fruit 68" x 71"

My quilt projects almost always start with the fabrics and colors. The New Quilts from an Old Favorite challenge is different because you are given a starting point with the traditional block that is chosen.

I divided the block into eight sections (meaning I could use more fabrics), turned the corner designs into curved leaves, extending them beyond the edges of the block, then rotated the orange and leaf design, moving the "navel" off-center.

I selected four sets of orange fabrics, plus green, a little purple, then black-and-white for punch, all tied together with the wonderful Guatemalan fabric I had purchased at the AQS show in Paducah.

I changed the background, then changed it again when I was arranging the blocks because I ran out of the wonderful purple and orange fabric. I added a hand-dyed bright orange fabric and put the orange "eyeball" fabric on top of it—one of my favorites that I have had for years. Now, it made sense to do the "oranges" in that section with the black-and-white fabrics.

More changes followed as I went along. Here's the final arrangement prior to sewing.

I did the orange blossoms with glue stick for placement and daisy stitch on the machine. It worked! They're not going anywhere.

Here's Marilyn, finishing up the quilting at the Houston Show. Gotta make that deadline!

Inspiration and Design: Marilyn

Claudia's quilts are always inspiring. Each one is a true original and as a result I am challenged to come up with original quilting. This keeps me on my toes and thinking about quilting in ways I would never think of with my own quilts.

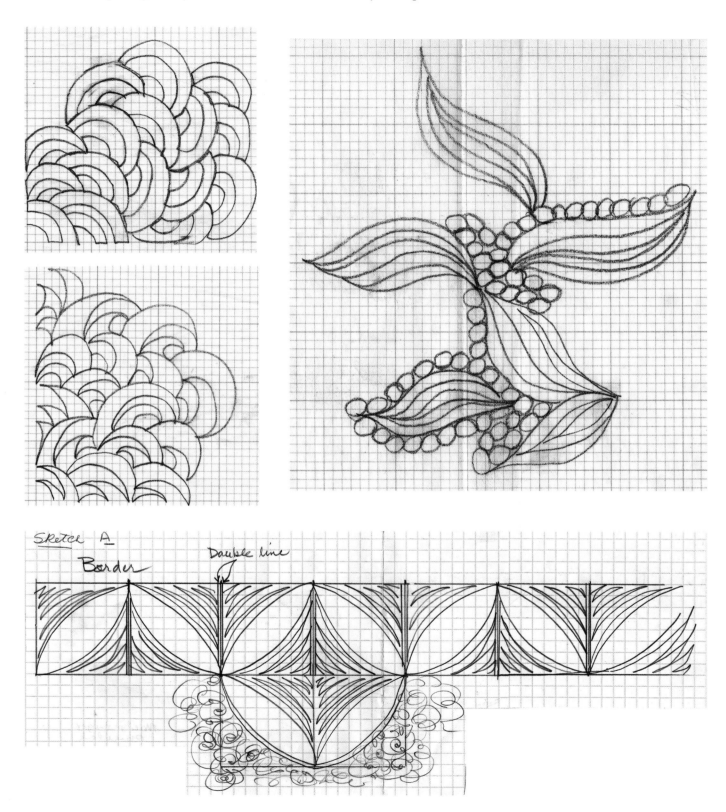

Technique

Here's the pattern for foundation of the Orange blocks. You can use a copier to increase or decrease the size. I used four different prints—two medium lights and two medium darks—alternating the light and dark placement around the shape. Use traditional foundation paper piecing on each half. Join the two halves, being careful to match the middle points. Press this seam open. Now, trim away the ¼" seam allowance on the paper only. Using the paper edge as a guide, fold the fabric over the edge to the back, all the way around the circle. Use spray starch if you like, or glue the folded edges in place, after you remove the paper.

Using your favorite machine-appliqué method, sew the pieced circle to a square piece of background fabric. Cut the block background fabric away behind the circle, leaving ¼" around the inside edge of the circle to reduce bulk, making the quilting easier.

Trace each rib onto template plastic with a permanent marker, numbering them as you go, and cut them out. Fuse paper-backed stabilizer to the back of your chosen rib fabrics. Using your templates—flipped over to the back—draw around each piece on the backing paper, again numbering each one as you go. Cut them out, remove the paper from one rib at a time, and fuse to the pieced foundation. Finish the edges using either a satin stitch or buttonhole stitch. The size and shape of the leaf templates can be varied.

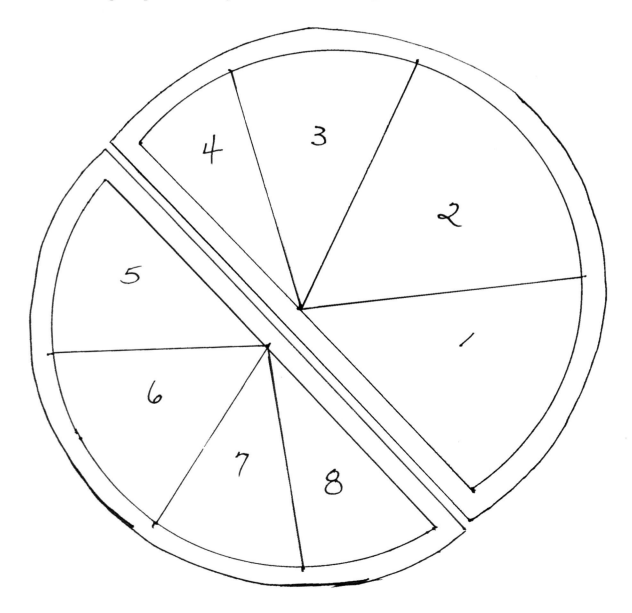

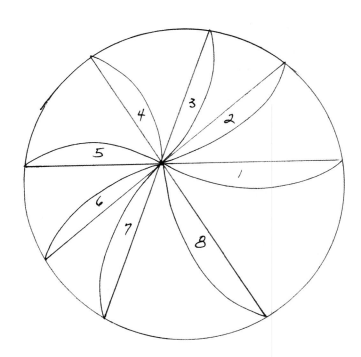

Finalists

Kathy McNeil
Marysville, Washington

Photo by Bruce McNeil

Geri Parker
Mt. Vernon, Washington

Meet Kathy & Geri

Geri had 10 minutes to make it to the post office with our CD and entry form this year. Seeing an American flag ahead, she made a screeching turn …into a funeral home, not the post office she expected! Thankfully, the post office let her in before locking the door. We both will work into the night if our daily goals have not been met. We hate being late. Both Geri and I set our clocks ten minutes ahead. This quilt started and finished behind schedule. Way behind schedule.

Geri sold her house after three years with no bites. She had to find a new house, pack up 23 years, and make a huge move. My daughter came home from Fairbanks with her 21-month-old daughter when complications in her second pregnancy forced her onto bed rest. Running after a two-year-old left me lots of extra quilting hours! The new baby came early, of course, and Geri kept saying, "Babies are more important than a contest, Kathy".

We fondly call our entry "Blood, Sweat, and Tears." Babies do keep things in perspective and life is full of unexpected changes. The single most important thing about our quilt is that we have a thousand little memories woven into it—every challenge, every "ah ha" moment. That is the thing we share the most. It's the journey we take together, laughing, teasing, occasionally swearing, and watching our husbands scratching their heads when they hear us completing each other's thoughts. One of my favorite memories is erupting into giggles after taking a picture of Geri's behind as she worked on our border. "It will be a great shot for the book," I told her. (A shot, mercifully, not included here.) The look she gave me could have made hell freeze over and still makes me laugh with delight.

I think that is why women have always made quilts together. There are little secrets in each quilt that only the makers know. Those stitches pulled us even closer together in friendship. We have been collaborating on one traditional quilt a year for five years now. Amazingly, they have all won awards. Geri sticks to piecing and I do the appliqué and quilting. Whenever we run into a challenge, Geri figures a way to piece us out of it or I resort to appliquéing over it. Somehow it all works out in the end. Simply by playing nicely together, we bring forth something of lasting value.

Inspiration and Design

The mission of The National Quilt Museum is: Explore the Vision, Advance the Art. Doing that requires looking back and looking forward. The earliest story to be found about the Orange Peel block calls it the Lafayette block. After a sumptuous dinner party in Philadelphia, a fair guest at his banquet took home a most beautiful fruit as her souvenir, an orange, imported from Barcelona. To preserve her treasure and the memory of gala days, a pattern was carefully made from the pared rind, which comes down to us as the Orange Peel quilt block.

The *French* connection was the jumping off platform for this design. A most royal quilt was called for. Something with the French royal colors perhaps? I Googled the image for the French Royal Coat of Arms—oh so pretty, a wine-colored burgundy, gold, and royal blue on a white background, with plenty of contrast to make it dramatic and interesting.

Fleur-de-Lis 68½" x 68½"

I think that is why women have always made quilts together. There are little secrets in each quilt that only the makers know.

We have a McNeil coat of arms hanging in my hallway and by comparison this one was really stunning. Five years ago we went on a family heritage tour of Scotland and later jumped across the pond to take in Versailles. It's a good thing we saw my husband's hovel of a castle in the Outer Hebrides before going there. Unable to take in the opulent paintings on the ceiling, I lay down on the floor for a better view. Instantaneously there was a guard there to tell me that was not allowed. The look he gave me made it quite clear that my manners were certainly not up to Versailles standards. Chagrined, I stood up and resisted the temptation to curtsey. It is an amazing place. The artwork, architecture, fiber arts, woodwork, and gardens have inspired many an artist for over a century.

I had the colors now. We could incorporate the fleur-de-lis—an instantly recognizable French symbol. Visions of gems and crystals bounced across my brain. Now to create an original elegant look for the traditional block. Two of the versions printed on the contest brochure caught my eye. One seemed to emphasize the points between the peels and one the elliptical shape of the peels. If we used contrasting colors for both of those features, we could combine the points and peels into one block. But it still needed a *new* look.

I love Shakespearean costumes and the little Cathedral Window effects sometimes seen in the sleeves are always my favorite. I tried arranging a diamond shape over the peel and left a cut-out window. Using my machine embroidery stitch, I decorated it further adding a fleur-de-lis in the center and some jewels for the final effect.

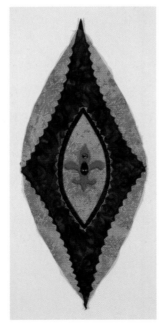

A 24" working center medallion was born, surrounded by four 8" identical blocks set on point. For variety and interest the four remaining 8" blocks were set square and finished differently. Finally some curved designs I call "flourishes" connected all the blocks. Forty 6" half-blocks made up the inner border.

Flourishes

Flourishes template

Geri and I specialize in original and creative border designs. I knew we needed something with freestanding points around the border, so Geri designed the curved border points reminiscent of scallops.

Techniques

Geri's specialty is piecing and mine is appliqué so our designs always incorporate both of those techniques. Geri began by drafting our innovative blocks on freezer paper. All of the blocks were constructed in the same manner, starting with foundation paper piecing and finishing with a dash of appliqué.

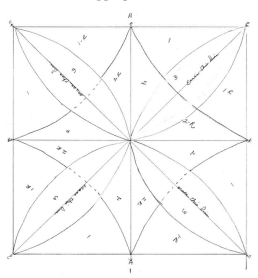

We drew a master pattern and made a copy to use for templates. Each shape was cut out accurately, traced face down on fabric, and cut out leaving at least ¼" seam allowance. I used a larger seam allowance on the small pieces and trimmed them after sewing for a more accurate fit.

The blocks were pieced and Cathedral Window diamonds were machine appliquéd on top with contrasting colored piping to create dimension and texture inside of each window. The blocks were appliquéd to the background fabric and connected with flourishes to add a great sense of motion around the quilt. Ten half-square blocks made up each inner border. Prior to quilting, we added trapunto quilting designs with water-soluble thread. The quilting was done before adding the final curved border.

To make our freestanding curved border peaks, measure the side of your quilt. Decide how large you would like each "curved border peak" unit to be. Divide the measurement by this number. Adjust the unit size up or down to allow a perfect fit.

Draw a gentle curve using a compass, plate, or other device to get a half curve. Make a paper template (I used freezer paper) the length of the quilt side. Place it against the edge of your quilt to check the fit. Cut two strips of fabric right sides together, with a fusible stabilizer on one fabric. Use the freezer-paper template to mark the curved edge with pencil, remove the freezer paper, sew along the marked line, and trim closely. Turn right-side out and press. Measure again against the side of the quilt.

Cut two 1" strips of fabric the length of the border unit—one matching the front of the quilt, one matching the back of the quilt. Sew each matching strip to the front and back of the border. Center the border along the edge and sew the front binding to the front of your quilt. Repeat for the other three sides, then hand finish the binding on the back. Press.

Finalist
Deborah Spofford
Shanghai, China

Photo by Sauchi Yong

Meet Deborah

Four years ago I moved to Shanghai, China, with my husband and daughter. Our son was attending university at the time and soon followed with an internship opportunity. Moving to China gave me the "gift of time" because many of my previous obligations and responsibilities suddenly ended. I enjoy working with textiles and creating things with fabric, so I used the time to seriously explore the art of quilting. My previous experience with quilting was very limited and usually happened once every five years during the Super Bowl when I pieced a small quilt top while everyone else watched the football game.

A few months after we settled in our Shanghai apartment, I encroached on my husband's office space. I found the perfect cutting table at an antique market and a cabinet to hold my very small stash of fabric. I found another narrow antique table to hold my sewing machines. It is a very small space but fairly efficient.

After I established a workspace, I scouted the fabric markets and started to experiment. I tried a variety of fabrics and techniques. I read several books about quilting and began teaching myself. I was blessed to find a quilt group in Shanghai that was not only diverse by nationality but also diverse by quilting styles. It was a wonderful environment to learn and create and eventually I became one of the teachers.

I attended various workshops during our home leave and continued to develop my skills. I taught classes in our apartment, and recently traveled to Korea to teach a quilting class at a women's university, but I still feel like a beginner. SHANGHAI LIGHTS is my first major piece and the first quilt that I entered in a juried show.

These are a few of the things that I learned about myself during the past four years as I learned to quilt:
• I would rather quilt than practice Mandarin.
• My favorite travel souvenir is fabric.
• 120 yards of fabric weighs exactly 20 kilograms and fits perfectly in my gray duffel bag.
• My sewing machines should have their own frequent flyer number.
• Security guards look perplexed when they discover I have a sewing machine in my carry-on bag.
• My favorite part of making a quilt is hand stitching the binding because I finally get to snuggle with it.
• I like to create designs on my computer and then make them a reality with my hands.
• I will never have enough time to make all the quilts that are in my imagination.

Before moving to China I worked in the hobby and leisure arts industry designing DIY projects and writing "how to" instructions for magazines and books. I also facilitated product education for several manufacturers and created and presented DIY projects on a morning television program in the Pacific Northwest. We will

Shanghai Lights 72" x 72"

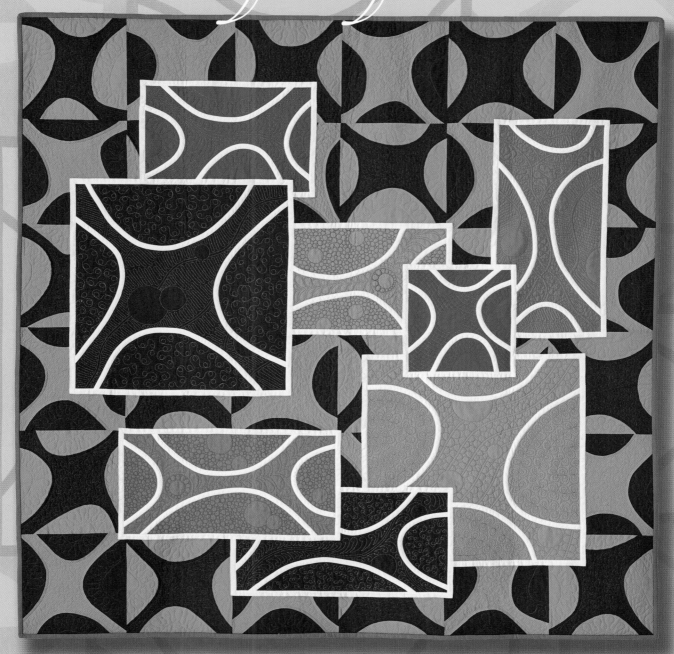

*My favorite part of making a quilt
is hand stitching the binding because
I finally get to snuggle with it.*

soon be moving back to the United States, and I plan to continue developing my quilting skills and to pursue a master's degree in textile design.

Inspiration and Design

Shanghai Lights was inspired by the bright colors that are visible from the 36th floor window of our home in China. The nighttime cityscape is beautiful with neon lights illuminating the buildings, bridges, ships, and roadways. I was inspired to make this quilt because my family will be leaving China soon and I wanted to commemorate our time here and showcase the quilting skills that I learned during the past four years.

I was challenged by the Orange Peel pattern because it is not one that I would normally choose. I wanted to answer a "what if" question—"What if the curves do not match?" I thought it would be interesting to stray from the rigid perfection that is often the goal when making this traditional block and to create something more playful. I also wanted to experiment with bias strips to create variations of the basic Orange Peel block.

Many things that are "made in China" are not actually available for sale in China. Good quality cotton fabrics are one of those items. I used solid color linen fabrics because they are easy to find in the textile markets. Linen was a good choice because the loosely woven texture adapted to the curves very nicely.

The original design for this quilt was sketched on paper and then rendered on my computer using Adobe® Illustrator® software. I found this process to be very helpful. I enjoyed having the ability to manipulate the design on the computer with many "what if" ideas. I saved

the design changes as I went along and then chose the one I liked the best. The computer-aided design also made it easy to create the scale for each of the blocks and worked as a visual template when I was constructing the background. I believe this saved a lot of time and fabric. I could easily tell which of the background blocks would be cut away later so I filled those spaces with white fabric instead of making an Orange Peel block that would eventually be wasted. Having the design on my computer was also very helpful when it came time to place the large blocks on the background.

It would be interesting to develop this design into a series by changing the shapes of the large blocks and introducing circles. Experimenting with the outside shape of the quilt would also be interesting. I would like to introduce shadows around the larger blocks and add different colors to the larger sections of the blocks. I liked working with bias strips and I look forward to experimenting more with them.

Techniques

Constructing the Background Blocks

It was important for the background blocks to lie very flat, and sometimes this can be a challenge when you are piecing curves. The process that worked best for me was to first cut and sew one set of curves on opposite sides of a block. After pressing the seams of the first two curves, I cut the arcs for the second set of curves. This helped keep the blocks flat and maintain the original shape of the block.

Making Bias Strips

I experimented with several different ways to press, turn, and stitch the bias strips. I found that it was easier to achieve a consistent width if I did not turn the seam allowance to the inside. This also allowed me to press the seam allowance flat and open. The bias strips were white and it was very noticeable if the seam allowance was not open or if it was twisted. If the fabric was a darker color this might not be a big problem.

Creating the Large Blocks

I cut the large blocks to the size specified by my rendering. I drew random curves on the blocks with a chalk pencil. Bias strips were placed over the lines and pressed to match the shape of the curve. The strips were machine basted to the block. Next a frame was created around the perimeter of the blocks. The corners of the frame were carefully mitered. The raw edges of each frame were turned and pressed under to create a crisp outer edge.

Assembling the Quilt

It was a challenge to organize the construction process of this quilt. I wanted the large blocks to float on the background, but this idea did not adapt well to a traditional grid. I thought it would be very difficult to inset the large blocks into the background. I solved this issue by first making the background blocks and sewing them together. In the areas that I knew would be covered by the large blocks I inserted plain white fabric "spacers."

The large blocks were then placed, pinned, and sewn to the background. The excess layers of background fabric behind the large blocks were cautiously cut away from the backside of the quilt top.

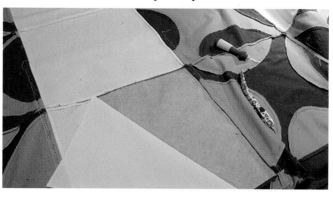

Free-Motion Quilting

I designed the large blocks to have copious open spaces for free-motion quilting. The quilting patterns emerged as I worked on the quilt. I started quilting the center large block and worked toward the edges of the quilt.

Finalists

Mary Sue Suit
Sidney, Nebraska

Photo by Judy Woodworth

Photo by Bill Woodworth

Judy Woodworth
Gering, Nebrasksa

Meet Mary Sue & Judy

One of the greatest joys of my life has been my friendship with Judy Woodworth. I consider her a wonderful gift. We have been making show quilts together since 2006. I have no idea how she puts up with me.

About ten years ago, Judy and I met at a quilt show sponsored by the Panhandle Quilt Guild in western Nebraska. I was working at the entrance table and she and her husband came to the show. It was the only function of the guild that I was able to attend that year so I believe fate brought us together. We exchanged some chit chat and found that she was new to the area and lived just a block from me at the time. Phone numbers crossed the table and a few days later I received a call from Judy and, my goodness, we were fast friends in a heartbeat.

Judy had just purchased her first longarm quilting machine, so I have had the pleasure of watching her skills and custom quilting business grow and of collaborating with her, something I hope will continue for many years to come. I am sure, though, that her greatest trial and challenge is living with the knowledge that Mary Sue will make the deadline but with very little time to spare.

Seldom knowing beforehand what the top looks like, she has by necessity become adept at the art of speed reading my quilt top and making it come alive with just the right quilting style and motifs. It has not been uncommon for Judy to begin the quilting design thought process based on a photo, only to find that the photo showed Plan A and the top delivered was Plan F. Yes, STAR-A-PEEL is indeed Plan F and it is very true that the quilting makes the quilt.

Design and Inspiration

Making a new quilt from this old favorite was a very difficult task for me as the Orange Peel block has long been on my "I'll never make this block" list. For some reason the traditional version of the block has never called to me. In truth when I first thought about entering this competition, all I could think of was what my daughter would say at the age of four: "I can't want to!"

As a result a great deal of time was spent just thinking about the block and mentally searching for a construction method that I could accept as a viable possibility. I needed to find a way to get rid of the "can't." There are several trial runs and designs in the Sidney, Nebraska, landfill, and I almost gave up entirely on the idea of completing a quilt top on which Judy could work her magic.

It was not until early October that I found a design and construction method I could enjoy and finish. The perseverance paid off and after a week and a half in the sewing room, the room was a disaster but a "big bang" had produced STAR-A-PEEL, a.k.a. LULU.

In the past I have been asked to describe my design process and methods. The truth is I have no organized method; everything occurs in the construction process as I simply react to what I have already done. I work with a quote from Pablo Picasso on my design wall, sent to me some years ago by my older sister. "If you know exactly what you are going to do—what is the point of doing it?" I like to think it validates my methods or the lack of the same. As a result, no sketches, in-progress patterns, photos, or notes exist.

Star~A~Peel 59½" x 59½"

The truth is I have no organized method;
everything occurs in the construction process
as I simply react to what I have already done.

LULU begins with one "traditional" Orange Peel block that explodes into a star shape created by triangles and diamonds, all within the melon-shaped border "peels" of four Orange Peel blocks. Each shape then contains the scallop peel of the traditional block.

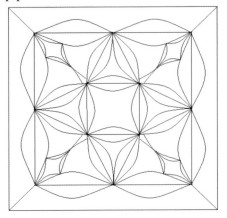

Technique

STAR-A-PEEL was constructed using a bias-appliqué technique for which narrow bias strips of the desired fabric are cut and applied to the edges of the design elements. The individual shapes are cut and layered so the correct order for applying the bias can be determined. The starting and stopping points for each strip application are important and must allow for covering the raw ends of the strips. These bias strips connect and secure the individual fabrics of each element. Once all the separate design elements have been created, they are in turn secured to each other with a bias strip, paying close attention to the start and stop points of each area.

The only traditional piecing occurs where the scalloped peel shapes are back-to-back. These are attached with bias strips as separate elements of the top.

The aspect of the bias technique that I find most interesting is the extra opportunity it affords for adding color to the design. It is possible to create highlights and shadows without adding extra pieces to each motif. This technique also creates added dimension to the surface of the quilt.

When Judy and I discussed the information for this section of the book, she said, "Well, I thought the top had an organic look so that is the style of quilting I used." That is stating it simply to say the least. The quilting in each area of the top is, in my estimation, as brilliant as any star in the sky. Judy used positive and negative areas of quilting to create texture and interest. Her use of contrasting thread colors allows the quilting to tell an integral part of the design story. From the consistent allover design in the lavender background to the more random and organic fill in the center block and diamond shards, the quilting emphasizes the big bang theory of the quilt.

Notice the lovely tangerine flowers in the aqua peels of the inner border. Who needs printed fabric when such a happy motif can be created by a quilting magician?

The dark blue outer border is filled with beautiful tangerine feathers with the contrasting thread completing the give-and-take aspect of the traditional block.

The top is finished with glass beads the same color as the quilting thread. They were applied randomly to appear as if they dropped off the thread during the quilting process, giving the quilt a little extra star shine.

Orange Peel Block Patterns

**A classic red-and-white version of Orange Peel
has also been called Turn About Quilt,
Pincushion, and Robbing Peter to Pay Paul**

Text for pages 88–92 based on information from *Encyclopedia of Pieced Patterns* by Barbara Brackman (AQS 1993)

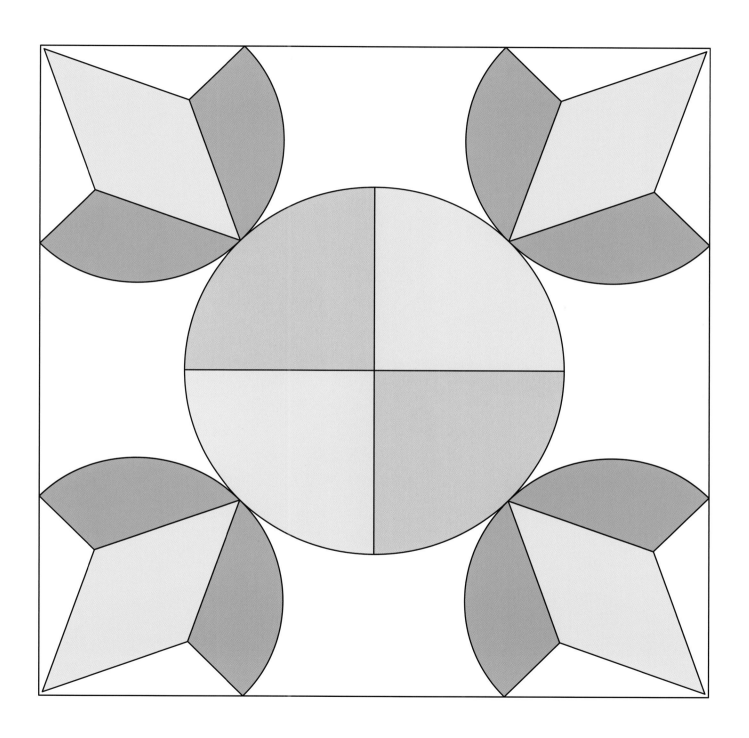

This appliqué version of Orange Peel appeared as a Grandma Dexter pattern in the 1930s.

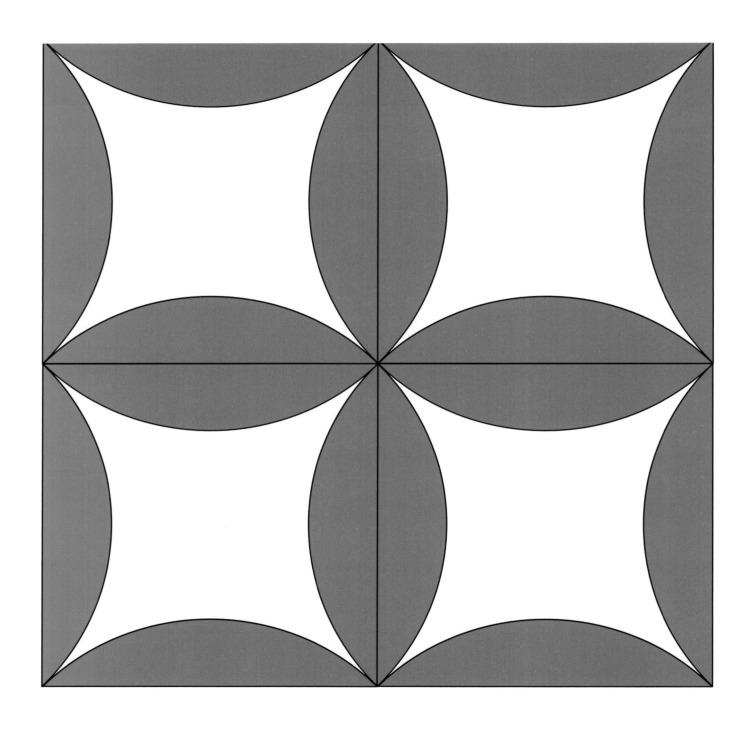

Is it Orange Peel or Cathedral Windows? Construction tells the difference for this block also known as Dolly Madison's Workbox, Love Ring, Sugar Bowl, and Mary's Choice.

**The timeless appeal of two-colored quilts is
apparent in this Orange Peel variation that
also looks like a Cathedral Window block.**

**Many names have been applied to this Orange Peel pattern:
Hickory Leaf, Job's Patience, The Reel, Compass,
Irish Chain, Orange Slices, and Oak Leaf.**

Resources

Books

Brackman, Barbara. *Encyclopedia of Pieced Quilt Patterns*. American Quilter's Society, 2003.

Lawler, Mickey. *Skydyes: A Visual Guide to Fabric Painting*. C&T Publishing, Inc., 1999.

Lewis, Alfred Allan. *The Mountain Artisans Quilting Book*. Macmillan Publishing Co., Inc., 1973. Includes the Rockefeller quilt, designed by Dorothy Weatherford of the West Virginia Mountain Artisans.

Magaret, Pat Maixner and Donna Ingram Slusser. *Watercolor Quilts*. That Patchwork Place, 1993.

Malone, Maggie. *5,500 Quilt Block Designs*. Sterling Publishing Co, Inc., 2003.

Stone, Karen K. *Karen K. Stone Quilts*. The Electric Quilt Company, 2004. This book has the Indian Orange Peel pattern.

Wells, Valori. *Radiant New York Beauties*. C&T Publishing, Inc., 2003.

Wolfrom, Joen. *Color Play: Easy Steps to Imaginative Color in Quilts*. C & T Publishing, Inc., 2000.

Quilters and Suppliers

Dharma Trading Company
Textile craft supplies & dyeables
www.dharmatrading.com

Elizaabeth's Studio
Fabric
www.elizabethsstudio.com

Karen K. Stone
Patterns
www.karenkstone.com

One Song Needle Arts
Statler Longarm Quilting Patterns for the artistic soul
www.onesongneedlearts.com

Polar Notions
Mini-bolts and circle templates
www.polarnotions.com

Renae Haddadin
Quilts on the Corner
Longarm quilting instruction and services
Amazing Rays® tools
www.renaequilts.com

Sally Terry
Longarm quilter
Terry Twist® patterns and templates
www.sallyterry.com

Software

Blender
Free open source 3-D content creation suite, available for all major operating systems under the GNU General Public License.
www.blender.org

CorelDRAW® X5
All-in-one graphics software suite
www.corel.com

The Electric Quilt Company
Quilt design software
www.electricquilt.com

The National Quilt Museum

Established in 1991 by American Quilter's Society (AQS) founders Bill and Meredith Schroeder as a not-for-profit organization, The National Quilt Museum is the world's foremost and largest museum devoted to quilts. Located in a 27,000 square foot facility in historic downtown Paducah, Kentucky, it is the only museum dedicated to today's quilts and quiltmakers. It was designed specifically to exhibit quilts aesthetically and safely. Three expansive galleries that surround visitors in color, design, and exquisite stitchery feature ten to twelve exhibits annually.

In July 1998, the United States Congress designated the Museum of the American Quilter's Society as The National Quilt Museum of the United States. While the designation does not come with federal funding, it provides national recognition of the museum's significance and stature as a national cultural and educational treasure.

The highlight of any visit is The William & Meredith Schroeder Gallery with a rotating exhibit of quilts from the museum's own collection of over 300 quilts. The nucleus of the collection is composed of extraordinary contemporary quilts collected privately by the Schroeders and donated to the museum. The collection continues to expand with the addition of purchase award quilts from the annual AQS Quilt Show & Contest and by purchase or donation of exceptional quilts selected to enhance the collection.

In 2006, *Oh Wow!*—a stunning collection of more than 40 miniature quilts—was added to the collection.

Educational programs offered in three well-equipped classrooms serve local and national audiences. The museum offers an annual schedule of in-depth workshops taught by

Teacher Laura Wasilowski with student. Photo by Susan Edwards.

Expanding the Vision, Advancing the Art

Photo by Charles R. Lynch

master quilters. Educational activities are also offered for youth including hands-on projects, summer quilt camps, a junior quilter and textile artist club, and the School Block Challenge contest open to students nationwide.

Exhibitions like *New Quilts from an Old Favorite*, developed by the museum, travel to other galleries and museums across the United States, helping to educate and inspire a broader spectrum of viewers.

The museum's bookstore has one of the largest selections of quilt books anywhere, with more than 700 quilt-related book titles available. In addition, the museum's shop offers quilts and quilt-related merchandise as well as fine crafts

Student with Phil Beaver. Photo by Susan Edwards.

by artisans from the region and beyond. The entire facility is wheelchair accessible.

The museum is open year-round from 10 a.m. to 5 p.m., Monday through Saturday, and from 1 p.m. to 5 p.m. on Sundays, April through October. Check the museum's website, www.quiltmuseum.org, for program information and extended hours during special events. For additional contact information, see Resources, page 93.

Photo by Charles R. Lynch

other AQS books

This is only a small selection of the books available from the American Quilter's Society. AQS books are known world-wide for timely topics, clear writing, beautiful color photos, and accurate illustrations and patterns. The following books are available from your local bookseller, quilt shop, or public library.

#8347	$24.95
#8355	$24.95
#7611	$26.95
#8349	$24.95
#8240	$26.95
#8346	$26.95
#8152	$26.95
#7926	$24.95
#8242	$22.95